Edward Caird

Essays on Literature and Philosophy

Edward Caird

Essays on Literature and Philosophy

ISBN/EAN: 9783337072599

Printed in Europe, USA, Canada, Australia, Japan

Cover: Foto ©ninafisch / pixelio.de

More available books at **www.hansebooks.com**

ESSAYS ON LITERATURE
AND PHILOSOPHY

BY

EDWARD CAIRD,

PROFESSOR OF MORAL PHILOSOPHY IN THE UNIVERSITY OF GLASGOW,
LATE FELLOW AND TUTOR OF MERTON COLLEGE, OXFORD,
AUTHOR OF "THE CRITICAL PHILOSOPHY OF IMMANUEL KANT."

VOL. II.

Glasgow
JAMES MACLEHOSE AND SONS
PUBLISHERS TO THE UNIVERSITY

1892

All rights reserved

CONTENTS.

CARTESIANISM.

GENERAL RELATIONS OF DESCARTES, MALEBRANCHE, AND SPINOZA.

1. *Descartes*—His Relation to the Reformers—His View of Doubt and his Method of Abstraction—Objections to the *Cogito ergo sum* and his Answers to them—Idea of God as the Link between the Subject and the Object—Its Priority to Both, and Difficulties thence arising—How Descartes avoids Pantheism—His Statement of the Ontological Argument—Unequal Relation of God to Matter and Mind—Absolute Arbitrariness of Will in God, and Relative Arbitrariness of Will in Man—The Idea of Matter and the Proof of its Existence—Mechanical View of Nature, and even of the Animal Organism—Explanation of the Feelings and Desires of Man—Occasional Causes—Ethical Views of Descartes—The Relation of Reason to Passion,   · · ·   Pp. 267—310.

2. *Malebranche*—General Character of his Development of the Cartesian Philosophy—Meaning of the Doctrine that we "see all things in God"—Existence of Things out of God—How we know ourselves—Approximation to the Pantheism which views God not as Spirit but as Substance—Attempt to reconcile this Philosophy with Christianity—Controversy with Arnauld as to a Particular Providence—The Love of God and its Relations to Other Loves—Effects of the Fall of Man—Tendency to Asceticism and Mysticism,   · · · · ·   Pp. 310—332.

3. *Spinoza*—His relation to Descartes and to the Jewish Philosophers—His Mathematical Method—Negation of the Finite as the Way

to Knowledge and Love of the Infinite—Distinction of Opinion and Knowledge—Abstractness of Opinion and its Dependence on Imagination—Knowledge based upon the Idea of God, or of Nature as a Whole—Distinction of *Ratio* and *Scientia Intuitiva*—Individuals reduced to Modes, and Mind and Matter to Attributes of the Infinite Substance—Consequences of the Principle that *Determinatio est negatio*—Disappearance of Evil *sub specie æternitatis*—Mind and Matter as Parallel Attributes—Relation of Soul and Body—Whether Spinoza's Distinction of Attributes is Relative to our Intelligence—Conflict of the Ideas of an Abstract and a Concrete Unity—Imperfect Return from the Infinite to the Finite—Ethical Consequences of Spinoza's Doctrine—Relation of the *Conatus sese conservandi* to the *Amor Dei Intellectualis*—Identification of Intelligence and Will—New Idea of Freedom—That Freedom is possessed by God, and may be shared by Man—His View of the Passions—His professed Rejection of Asceticism, and indirect Admission of it as an *Element* in Morality—Whether he admits Degrees in Existence—His Influence on Later Philosophy, ... Pp. 332—383.

METAPHYSIC.

Introduction—Origin of the Term—Aristotle's Account of it, as the Science of the First Principles of Being and Knowing, and as the Science of God—Fourfold Aspect of Metaphysic in Relation (1) to Science in General, (2) to Psychology, (3) to Logic, and (4) to Philosophy of Religion, ... Pp. 384—392.

1. *Relation of Metaphysic to Science*—Abstract Principles of Early Greek Philosophy—Advance of Socratic School to a Systematic Philosophy—Difference between Plato and Aristotle as to the Relation of the Individual and the Universal—Mediæval Realism and Nominalism—Nominalism and Empiricism of Bacon and his Successors—Mr. Spencer's Attempt to explain the existence of an *a priori* Element in Experience—Kant's view of the *A priori*—Why he limits Knowledge to Phenomenal Objects, while Thought is Extended to Noumena—Change in the Meaning of this Distinction is the Dialectic—Function of the Ideas of Reason—The Practical Faith of the *Critique of Practical Reason*—

Connection established between the Phenomenal and Intelligible Worlds in the *Critique of Judgment*—Necessary Divergence of the Interpreters of Kant, Fichte, Schelling and Hegel—Hegel's View of the Relation of Philosophy to Science, Pp. 392—442.

2. *Relation of Metaphysic to Psychology.*—Locke's Psychological Criticism of Knowledge—Results of the Confusion of the Psychological and the Metaphysical Problems—Man as a Subject of Knowledge and yet a Particular Object—Socratic View of the Universal as presupposed in the Consciousness of the Particular—Plato's Doctrine of Reminiscence and Right Opinion—Aristotle's Combination of Empiricism with the Doctrine that Reason is potentially all it thinks—His Admission of an absolute *A posteriori* which is not thinkable—Mediæval Compromise between Faith and Reason—Protestant Principle of Subjectivity in Religion and Bacon's Objective Principle in Science—How they correct each other—Compromise between the *A priori* and the *A posteriori*—Rejection of this Compromise from different sides by Locke and Leibniz—Their Reconciliation under the Doctrine of Development—How Kant prepares the way for it—Defect of the Darwinian View of Development—Relation of the Progressive Knowledge of the Individual to the Idea of Knowledge—How he transcends his own Limits—Possibility of Metaphysic as determining the First and Final Cause of Things,
Pp. 442—480.

3. *Relation of Metaphysic to Logic*—Separation of Logic from Metaphysic—Its Derivation from Aristotle—Its Appearance in Scholasticism and in Baconian Empiricism—Aristotle's Real Doctrine—Impossibility of Separating the Form from the Matter of Thought—What is meant by the Exclusion of Subjective Idola in Science—Passivity and Activity of the Mind—Aristotle's Attempt at a Synthetic Logic in the *Posterior Analytics*—His View of the Unity of Self-consciousness—His Vindication of the Principle of Contradiction—Necessity of a Complementary Principle of Relation—The Three Logics: the formal Logic of Analysis, the real Logic of External Synthesis, and the Genetic Logic, as representing three stages in the Process of Science—How Hume and Kant explain the Logic of Synthesis, and lead on to the Genetic

Logic, which is ruled by the Categories of Organic Unity and Development—Reconciliation of the Opposition between *A priori* and *A posteriori*—Unity of Logic and Metaphysic, Pp. 480—512.

4. *Relation of Metaphysic to Philosophy of Religion*—That a First Principle must also be a Last Principle—That a True Metaphysic must be able to explain Religion—Why certain Philosophies cannot do so—Essential Identity of Principle in Aristotle's *Metaphysic* and Hegel's *Logic*—Self-consciousness as the type of Knowledge—Relation of it to the Consciousness of the External World—Objections to Hegel's Step from Logic to the Philosophy of Nature—Cartesian Opposition of Mind and Matter—Its Reappearance in Mr. Spencer's Philosophy—Mind as transcending its own Distinction from Matter—The Subjective Synthesis of Comte an Illogical Compromise—Impossibility of Religion under it—That Religion implies a Unity of Principle in Nature and Spirit—Connection of Idealism with Christianity—The Possibility of Metaphysic, - - - - - - - - Pp. 512—539.

CARTESIANISM.

BY Cartesianism is here meant the philosophy developed in the works of Des Cartes, Malebranche, and Spinoza. It is impossible to exhibit the full meaning of these authors except in their relation to each other, for they are all ruled by one and the same thought in different stages of its evolution. It may be true that Malebranche and Spinoza were prepared, the former by the study of Augustine, the latter by the study of Jewish philosophy, to draw from Cartesian principles consequences which Des Cartes never anticipated. But the foreign light did not alter the picture on which it was cast, but only let it be seen more clearly. The consequences were legitimately drawn. It may be shown that they lay in the system from the first, and that they were evolved by nothing but its own immanent dialectic. At the same time, it is not likely that they would ever have been brought into such clear consciousness, or expressed with such consistency, except by a philosopher whose circumstances and character had completely detached him from all the convictions and prejudices of the age. In Malebranche, Cartesianism found an interpreter whose meditative spirit was fostered by the cloister, but whose speculative boldness was restrained by the traditions of the Catholic church. In Spinoza it found one who was in spirit and position more completely isolated than any monk, who was removed from the influence of the religious as well as the secular world of his time, and who in his solitude seemed scarcely ever to hear any voice but the voice of philosophy. It is because Cartesianism found such a pure organ of expression that its development is, in some sense, complete and typical. Its principles have been carried to their ultimate result, and we have before us all the data necessary to determine their value.

Des Cartes was, in the full sense of the word, a partaker of the modern spirit. He was equally moved by the tendencies that produced the Reformation, and the tendencies that produced the revival of letters and science. Like Erasmus and Bacon, he sought to escape from a transcendent and unreal philosophy of the other world to a knowledge of man and of the world in which he lives. But, like Luther, he found within human experience, among the matters nearest to man, the consciousness of God, and therefore his renunciation of scholasticism did not end either in materialism or in that absolute distinction between faith and reason which inevitably leads to the downfall of faith. What was peculiar to Des Cartes, however, was the speculative interest which made it impossible for him to rest in mere experience, whether of things spiritual or things secular, without searching, both in our consciousness of God and also in our consciousness of the world, for the links by which they are bound to the consciousness of self. In both cases it is his aim to go back to the beginning, to retrace the unconscious process by which the world of experience was built up, to discover the hidden logic that connects the different parts of the structure of belief, and to substitute a reasoned system, all whose elements are interdependent, for an unreasoned congeries of opinions. Hence his first step involves reflection, doubt, and abstraction. Turning the eye of reason upon itself, he tries to measure the value of that collection of beliefs of which he finds himself possessed ; and the first thing that reflection seems to discover is its accidental and uncon-. nected character. It is a mass of incongruous materials, accumulated without system and untested. Its elements have been put together under all kinds of influences, without any conscious intellectual process, and therefore we can have no assurance of their reality. In order that we may have such assurance, we must unweave the web of experience and thought which we have first woven in our sleep, that we may begin at the beginning and weave it over again with "clear and distinct" consciousness of what we are doing. *De omnibus dubitandum est.* We must free ourselves by one decisive effort from the weight of custom, prejudice, and tradition with which our consciousness of the world has been overlaid, that in that consciousness in its simplest and most elementary form we may find the true beginning of knowledge.

The method of doubt is at the same time a method of abstraction, by which Des Cartes rises above the thought of the particular objects of knowledge, in order that he may find the primary truth in which lies the very definition of knowledge, or the reason why anything can be said to be true. First disappears the whole mass of dogmas and opinions as to God and man which are confessedly received on mere authority. Then the supposed evidence of sense is rejected, because external reality is not immediately given in sensation. It is acknowledged by all that the senses often mislead us as to the nature of the things without us, and perhaps they may also mislead us as to there being anything without us at all. Nay, by a stretch of effort, we can carry doubt beyond this point, we can doubt even mathematical truth. When, indeed, we have our thoughts directed to the geometrical demonstration, when the steps of the process are immediately before our minds, we cannot but assent to the proposition that the angles of a triangle are equal to two right angles; but when we forget or turn away our thoughts from such demonstration, we can imagine that God or some powerful spirit is playing upon our minds to deceive them, so that even our most certain judgments may be illusory.

In this naïve manner does Des.Cartes express the idea that there are necessities of thought prior to, and presupposed in, the truth of geometry. He is seeking to strip thought of all the "lendings" that seem to come to it from anything but itself, of all relation to being that can be supposed to be given to it from without, that he may discover the primary unity of thought and being on which all knowledge depends. And this he finds in pure self-consciousness. Whatever I abstract from, I cannot abstract from self, from the "I think" that, as Kant puts it, "accompanies all our ideas"; for it was just the independence of this universal element in relation to the particulars that made all our previous abstraction possible. Even doubt rests on certitude; alone with self I cannot get rid of this self. By an effort of thought I separate my thinking self from all that I think, but the thinking self remains, and in thinking I am. *Cogito ergo sum.* The objective judgment of self-consciousness is bound up with or involved in the very faculty of judging, and therefore remains when we abstract from all other objective judgments. It is an assertion involved in the very process by which we dismiss all other assertions. Have we not then a right to regard it as a primitive unity of thought and being, in which is contained, or out of which may be developed, the very definition of truth?

The sense in which Des Cartes understood his first principle becomes clearer when we look at his answers to the objections made against it. On the one hand it was challenged by those who asked, like Gassendi, why the argument should be based especially on thought, and why we might not say with as good a right *ambulo ergo sum*. Des Cartes explains that it is only as referred to consciousness that walking is an evidence of my existence; but if I say "I am conscious of walking, therefore I exist," this is equivalent to saying, "I think in one particular way, therefore I exist." But it is not thinking in a particular way, but thinking in general that is co-extensive with my existence. I am not always conscious of walking, or of any other special state or object, but I am always conscious; for except in consciousness there is no ego, and where there is consciousness there is always an ego. Do I then always think, even

s

in sleep, asks the objector; and Des Cartes exposes himself to the criticisms of Locke by answering that it is impossible that there should ever be an interval in the activity of consciousness, and by insisting that, as man is essentially a thinking substance, the child thinks, or is self-conscious, even in its mother's womb. The difficulty disappears when we observe that the question as to the conditions under which self-consciousness is developed in the individual human subject, does not affect the nature of self-consciousness in itself, or in its relation to knowledge. The force of Des Cartes's argument really lies in this, that the world as an intelligible world exists only for a conscious self, and that therefore the unity of thought and being which is realised in self-consciousness is the presupposition of all knowledge. Of this self it is true to say that it exists only as it thinks, and that it thinks always. *Cogito ergo sum* is, as Des Cartes points out, not a syllogism, but the expression of an identity which is discerned by the simple intuition of the mind.[1] If it were

[1] *Resp. ad secundas objectiones*, 74. I quote from the Elzevir edition.

otherwise, the major "*omne quod cogitat existit*" would require to have been known before the minor "*cogito*"; whereas, on the contrary, it is from the immediate consciousness of being as contained in self-consciousness that that major can alone be derived. Again, when Hobbes and others argued that thinking is, or may be, a property of a material substance, Des Cartes answers that the question whether the material and the thinking substance are one does not meet us at the outset, but can only be solved after we have considered what is involved in the conception of those different substances respectively.[1] In other words, to begin by treating thinking as a quality of a material substance is to go outside of the intelligible world for an explanation of the intelligible world. It is to ask for something prior to that which is first in thought. If it be true that the consciousness of self is that from which we cannot abstract, that which is involved in the knowledge of any object whatever, then to go beyond it and seek for a reason or explanation of it in anything else,

[1] *Resp. ad tertias objectiones,* 04

is to go beyond the beginning of knowledge; it is to ask for a knowledge before knowledge.

Des Cartes, however, is himself unfaithful to this point of view; for, strictly taken, it would involve the consequence, not only that there is nothing prior to the pure consciousness of self, but that there can be no object which is not in necessary relation to it. Hence there can be no absolute opposition between thought and anything else, no opposition which thought itself does not transcend. But Des Cartes commits the error of making thought the property of a substance, a *res cogitans*, which as such can immediately or directly apprehend nothing but thoughts or ideas; while, altogether outside of these thoughts and ideas, there is another substance which is characterised by the property of extension, and with which thought has nothing to do. Matter in space is thus changed, in Kantian language, into "a thing in itself," an object out of all relation to the subject; and, on the other hand, mind seems to be shut up in the magic circle of its own ideas, without any capacity of breaking out or apprehending any reality but itself. Between thought and being, in spite of their *subjective* unity in self-consciousness, a great gulf seems still to be fixed, which cannot be crossed, unless thought should become extended, or matter think. But to Des Cartes the dualism is absolute, because it is a presupposition with which he starts. Mind cannot go out of itself, cannot deal with anything but thought, without ceasing to be mind; and matter must cease to be matter ere it can lose its absolute externality, its nature as having *partes extra partes*, and acquire the unity of mind. They are opposed as the divisible and the indivisible, and there is no possible existence of matter in thought except a representative existence. The ideal (or, as Des Cartes calls it, objective) existence of matter *in* thought, and the real (or, as Des Cartes calls it, formal) existence of matter *out of* thought, are absolutely different and independent things.

It was, however, impossible for Des Cartes to be content with a subjective idealism that confined all knowledge to the tautological expression of self-consciousness: "I am I," "What I perceive I perceive." If the individual is to find in self-consciousness the principle of all knowledge, there must be something in that consciousness which transcends the distinction of self and not self, which carries him beyond the limit of his own individuality. What, then, is the point where the subjective consciousness passes out into the objective, from which it seemed at first absolutely excluded? Des Cartes answers that it is through the connection of the consciousness of self with the consciousness of God. It is because we find God in our minds that we find anything else. The proof of God's existence is the hinge on which the whole Cartesian philosophy turns. It is therefore necessary, before going farther, to examine somewhat closely the nature of that proof.

Des Cartes, in the first place, tries to extract a criterion of truth out of the *cogito ergo sum*. Why am I assured of my own existence? It is because the conception of existence is at once and immediately involved in the consciousness of self. I can logically distinguish the two elements, but I cannot separate them; whenever I clearly and distinctly conceive the one, I am forced to think the other along with it. But this gives me a rule for all judgments whatever, a principle which is related to the *cogito ergo sum* as the formal to the material principle of knowledge. Whatever we cannot separate from the clear and distinct conception of anything necessarily belongs to it in reality; and, on the other hand, whatever we can separate from the clear and distinct conception of anything does not necessarily belong to it in reality. Let us therefore set an object clearly before us, let us sever it in thought so far as is possible from all other objects, and we shall at once be able to determine what properties and relations are essential, and what are not essential to it. And if we find empirically that any object manifests a property or relation not involved in the clear and distinct conception of it, we can say with certainty that such property or relation does not belong to it except by arbitrary arrangement, or, in other words, by the external combination of things which in their own nature have no affinity or connection.

Now, by the application of this principle, we might at once assure ourselves of many mathematical truths; but, as has been already shown, there is a point of view from which we may doubt even these, so long as the idea of a God that deceives us is not excluded. If it is not certain that there is a God who cannot lie, it is not certain that there is an objective matter in space to which mathematical truth applies. But the existence of

God may be proved in two ways. In the first place, it may be proved through the principle of causality, which is a self-evident principle. We have in our mind many ideas, and, according to the principle of causality, all these ideas must be derived from something that contains a "formal" reality which corresponds to their "objective" reality, *i.e.*, which contains at least as much reality in its existence *out of* thought as they contain in their existence *in* thought. Now, we might derive from ourselves not only the ideas of other minds like ourselves, but possibly also the ideas of material objects; for such objects are lower in the scale of existence than ourselves, and therefore the ideas of them might be got by omitting some of the qualities which distinguish ourselves. But the idea of God, of a Being who is eternal and immutable, all-powerful, all-wise, and all-good, cannot be derived from our own limited and imperfect existence. Its origin, therefore, must be sought in a Being who contains actually in Himself all that is contained in our idea of Him.

To this argument it was objected by some of the critics of Des Cartes that the idea of God as the infinite Being is merely negative, and that it is derived from the finite simply by abstracting from its conditions. Des Cartes answers that the case is just the reverse; the infinite is the positive idea, and the finite is the negative, and it is therefore the former which is the presupposition of the latter. As Kant, at a later date, pointed out that space is not a general conception, abstracted from the ideas of particular spaces, and representing the common element in them; but that, on the contrary, the ideas of particular spaces are got by the limitation of the one infinite space which is prior to them, so Des Cartes maintains that the idea of the finite is attained by limitation of the infinite, and not the idea of the infinite by abstraction from the particular determinations of the finite. It is a necessary consequence of this that the self-consciousness of a finite being presupposes the consciousness of the infinite. Hence the idea of God is not merely one among the other ideas which we have, but it is the one idea that is necessary to our very existence as thinking beings, the idea through which alone we can think ourselves, or anything else. "It ought never to be supposed," says Des Cartes, "that the conception of the infinite is a negative idea, got by negation of the finite, just as I conceive repose to be merely negation of movement, and darkness merely the negation of light. On the contrary, I see manifestly that there is more reality in the infinite than in the finite substance, and that therefore I have in me the notion of the infinite, *even in some sense prior to the notion of the finite*, or, in other words, that the notion of myself in some sense presupposes the notion of God; for how could I doubt or desire, how could I be conscious of anything as a want, how could I know that I am not altogether perfect, if I had not in me the idea of a Being more perfect than myself, by comparison with whom I recognise the defects of my own existence?"[1] Des Cartes then goes on to illustrate in various ways the thesis that the consciousness of a defective and growing nature cannot give rise to the idea of infinite perfection, but, on the contrary, presupposes it. We could not think of a series of approximations, unless there were somehow present to us the idea of the completed infinite as the goal at which we aim. If we had not the consciousness of ourselves as finite *in relation* to the infinite, either we should not be conscious of ourselves at all, or we should be conscious of ourselves as

[1] *Meditatio tertia.*

infinite. The image of God is so impressed by Him upon us that we "conceive that resemblance wherein the idea of God is contained by the same faculty whereby we are conscious of ourselves." In other words, our consciousness of ourselves is at the same time consciousness of our finitude, and hence of our relation to a being who is infinite.

The principle which underlies the reasoning of Des Cartes is, that to be conscious of a limit is to transcend it. We could not feel the limits either upon our thought or upon our existence, we could not doubt or desire, if we did not already apprehend something beyond these limits. Nay, we could not be conscious of our existence as individual selves, unless we were conscious of that which is not ourselves, and of a unity in which both self and not-self are included. Our individual life is therefore to us, as self-conscious beings, a part of a wider universal life. Doubt and aspiration are but the manifestation of the essential division and contradiction of a nature, which, as conscious of itself, is at the same time conscious of the whole of which it is a part. And as the existence of a self and its consciousness are one, so we may say that a thinking being is not only an individual, but always in some sense identified with that universal unity of being to which it is essentially related.

If Des Cartes had followed out this line of thought, he would have been led at once to the pantheism of Spinoza, if not beyond it. As it is, he is on the verge of contradiction with himself when he speaks of the consciousness of God as *in some sense* prior to the consciousness of self. How can anything be prior to the first principle of knowledge? It is no answer to say that the consciousness of God is the *principium essendi*, while the consciousness of self is the *principium cognoscendi*. For, if the idea of God is prior to the idea of self, knowledge must begin where existence begins, with God. The words "in some sense," with which Des Cartes qualifies his assertion of the priority of the idea of God, only betray his hesitation and his partial consciousness of the contradiction in which he is involved. Some of Des Cartes's critics presented this difficulty to him in another form, and accused him of reasoning in a circle, when he said that it is because God cannot lie that we are certain that our clear and distinct ideas do not deceive us. The very existence of the conscious self, the *cogito ergo sum*, which is the first of all truths, and therefore prior in certitude to the existence of God, is believed only because of the clearness and distinctness with which we apprehend it. How, then, they asked, can God's truthfulness be our security for a principle which we must use in order to prove the being of God? The answer of Des Cartes is somewhat lame. We cannot doubt any self-evident principle, or even any truth based on a self-evident principle, when we are directly contemplating it in all the necessity of its evidence; it is only when we forget or turn away from this evidence, and begin to think of the possibility of a deceitful God, that a doubt arises which cannot be removed except by the conviction that God is true.[1] It can scarcely be said this is a *dignus vindice nodus*, or that God can fitly appear as a kind of second-best resource to the forgetful spirit which has lost its direct hold on truth and its faith in itself. God, truth, and the human spirit are thus conceived as having merely external and accidental relations with each other. What Des Cartes, however, is really expressing in this exoteric way is simply

[1] *Resp. quartæ*, 234.

that, beneath and beyond all particular truths, there lies the great general truth of the unity of thought and existence. In contemplating a particular truth, we may not consciously relate it to this unity, but when we have to defend it against scepticism we are forced to realise this relation. The ultimate answer to any attack upon a special aspect or element of truth must be to show that the fate of truth itself, the possibility of knowledge, is bound up with it, or, in other words, that we cannot doubt it without doubting reason itself. But to doubt reason is, in the language of Des Cartes, to doubt the truthfulness of God; for, in his view, the idea of God is involved in the very constitution of reason. Taken in this way, the import of Des Cartes's answer is, that the consciousness of self, like every other particular truth, is not at first seen to rest on the consciousness of God, but that when we realise what it means we see that it does so rest. But if this be so, then in making the consciousness of self his first principle of knowledge Des Cartes has stopped short of the truth. It can be the first principle only if it is understood, not as the consciousness of the individual self, but in a sense in which the consciousness of self is identical with the consciousness of God.

Des Cartes, however, is far from a clear apprehension of the ultimate unity of thought and being, which, nevertheless, he strives to find in God. Beginning with an absolute separation of the *res cogitans* from the *res extensa*, he is continually falling back into dualism just when he seemed to have escaped from it. Even in God the absolute unity, idea and reality fall asunder; our idea of God is not God in us, it is only an idea of which God's existence is the cause. But the category of causality, if it forms a bridge between different things, as here between knowing and being, at the same time repels them from each other. It is a category of external relation, which may be adequate to express the relation of the finite to the finite, but not the relation of the finite to the infinite. We cannot conceive God simply as the cause of our idea of Him, without making God a purely objective and therefore finite existence.

Nor is the case better when we turn to the so-called ontological argument,—that existence is necessarily involved in the idea of God, just as the property of having its angles equal to two right angles is involved in the idea of a triangle. If, indeed, we could take this as meaning that thought transcends the distinction between itself and existence, and that therefore existence cannot be a thing in itself out of thought, but must be an intelligible world that exists as such only for the thinking being, there would be some force in the argument. But this meaning we cannot find in Des Cartes, or to find it we must make him inconsistent with himself. He was so far from having quelled the phantom "thing in itself" that he treated matter in space as such a thing, and thus confused externality of space with externality to the mind. On this dualistic basis the ontological argument becomes a manifest paralogism, and lies open to all the objections that Kant brought against it. That the idea of God involves existence proves only that God, if He exists at all, exists by the necessity of His being. But the link that is to bind thought to existence is still wanting, and, in consistency with the other presuppositions of Des Cartes, it cannot be supplied.

But, again, even if we allow to Des Cartes that God is the unity of thought and being, we must still ask what is the nature of this unity? Is it a mere generic unity, reached by abstraction, and which therefore leaves out of account all the distinguishing characteristics of the particulars under it? Or is it a concrete unity to which the particular elements are subordinated, but in which they are nevertheless included? To answer this question we need only look at the relation of the finite to the infinite, as it is expressed in the passage already quoted, and in many others. Des Cartes always speaks of the infinite as a purely affirmative or positive existence, and of the finite, in so far as it is distinguished from the infinite, as purely negative, or, in other words, as a nonentity. "I am," he says, "a mean between God and nothing, between the Supreme Being and not-being. In so far as I am created by God, there is nothing in me that can deceive me or lead me into error. But, on the other hand, if I consider myself as participating in nothingness, or not-being, inasmuch as I am not myself the Supreme Being, but in many ways defective, I find myself exposed to an infinity of errors. Thus error as such is not something real that depends on God, but simply a defect; I do not need to explain it by means of any special faculty bestowed on me by God, but merely by the fact that the faculty for discerning truth from error with which He has endowed me, is not infinite."[1] But if we follow out this principle to its logical result, we must say not only that error is a consequence of finitude, but also that the very *existence* of the finite as such is an error or illusion. All finitude, all determination, according to the well-known Spinozistic aphorism, is negation, and negation cannot constitute reality. To know the reality of things, therefore, we have to abstract from their limits: therefore the only reality is the infinite. Finite being, *qua* finite, has no existence, and finite self-consciousness, consciousness of a self in opposition to, or limited by, a not-self is an illusion. But Des Cartes does not thus reason. He does not see "anything in the nature of the infinite which should exclude the existence of finite things." "What," he asks, "would become of the power of that imaginary infinite if it could create nothing? Perceiving in ourselves the power of thinking, we can easily conceive that there should be a greater intelligence elsewhere. And even if we should suppose that

---

[1] *Meditatio quarta.*

intelligence increased *ad infinitum*, we need not fear that our own would be lessened. And the same is true of all other attributes which we ascribe to God, even of His power, provided only that we do not suppose that the power in us is not subjected to God's will. In all points, therefore, He is infinite without any exclusion of created things."[1] The truth of this view we need not dispute; the question is as to its consistency with Cartesian principles. It may be a higher idea of God to conceive Him as revealing Himself in and to finite creatures; but it is a different idea from that which is implied in Des Cartes' explanations of error. It is an inconsistency that brings Des Cartes nearer to Christianity, and nearer, it may also be said, to a true metaphysic; but it is not the less an inconsistency with his fundamental principles, which must necessarily disappear in their subsequent development. To conceive the finite as not constituted merely by the absence of some of the positive elements of the infinite, but as in necessary unity with the infinite; to conceive the infinite as not merely that which has no limits, or determinations, but as that which is self-

[1] *Resp. ad. sec. object.*, p. 75.

determined and self-manifesting, which through all finitude and manifestation returns upon itself, may not be erroneous. But it would not be difficult to show that the adoption of such a conception involves the rejection or modification of almost every doctrine of the Cartesian system.

— In connection with this inconsistency we may notice the very different relations in which Des Cartes conceives mind on the one side and matter on the other to stand towards God, who yet is the cause of both, and must therefore, by the principle of causality, contain in Himself all that is in both. Matter and mind are to Des Cartes absolute opposites. Whatever can be asserted of mind can be denied of matter, whatever can be asserted of matter can be denied of mind. Matter is passive, mind is active; matter is extended, and therefore divisible *ad infinitum;* mind is an indivisible unity. In fact, though of this Des Cartes is not conscious, the determination of the one is mediated by its opposition to the other; the ideas of object and subject, the self and not-self, are terms of a relation distinguishable but inseparable. But in the idea of God we must find a unity which transcends this difference in one way or another, whether by combining the two under a higher notion, or, as it would be more natural to expect on Cartesian principles, by abstracting equally from the particular characteristics of both. Des Cartes really does neither, or rather he acts partly on the one principle and partly on the other. In his idea of God he abstracts from the properties of matter but not from those of mind. "God," he says, "contains in Himself *formaliter* all that is in mind, but only *eminenter* all that is in matter";[1] or, as he elsewhere expresses it more popularly, He *is* mind, but He is only the creator of matter. And for this Des Cartes gives as his reason that matter, as being divisible and passive, is essentially imperfect. *Ipsa natura corporis multas imperfectiones involvit*, and, therefore, "there is more analogy between sounds and colours than there is between material things and God." But the real imperfection here lies in the abstractness of the Cartesian conception of matter as merely extended, merely passive; and this is balanced by the equal abstractness of the conception of mind or self-consciousness as an absolutely simple activity, a pure intelligence without any object but itself. If matter as

[1] *Resp. ad. sec. object.*, 72-73.

absolutely opposed to mind is imperfect, mind as absolutely opposed to matter is also imperfect. In fact, they are the elements or factors of a unity, and lose all meaning when severed from each other, and if we are to seek this unity by abstraction, we must equally abstract from both.

The result of this one-sidedness is seen in the fact that Des Cartes, who begins by separating mind from matter, ends by finding the essence of mind in pure will, *i.e.*, in pure formal self-determination. Hence God's will is conceived as absolutely arbitrary, not determined by any end or law; for all laws, even the necessary truths that constitute reason, spring from God's determination, and do not precede it. "He is the author of the essence of things no less than their existence," and His will has no reason but His will. In man there is an intelligence with eternal laws or truths involved in its structure, which so far limits his will. "As man finds the nature of good and truth already determined by God, *his* will cannot be moved by anything else." His highest freedom consists in having his will determined by a clear perception of the nature of good and truth, and "he is never indifferent except when he is ignorant of it, or, at least, does not see it so clearly as to be lifted above the possibility of doubt."[1] Indifference of will is to him "the lowest grade of liberty," yet, on the other hand, in nothing does the image of God in him show itself more clearly than in the fact that his will is not limited by his clear and distinct knowledge, but is "in a manner infinite." For "there is no object of any will, even the infinite will of God, to which our will does not extend."[2] Belief is a free act, for as we can yield our assent to the obscure conceptions presented by sense and the imagination, and thus allow ourselves to be led into error, so, on the other hand, we can refuse to give this assent, or to allow ourselves to be determined by anything but the clear and distinct ideas of intelligence. That which makes it possible for us to err is that also in which the divine image in us is most clearly seen. We cannot have the freedom of God, whose will creates the object of His knowledge; but in reserving our assent for the clear and distinct perceptions of intelligence we, as it were, re-enact for ourselves the divine law, and repeat, so far as is possible to finite beings, the

[1] *Resp. Sextæ;* 160-163.   [2] *Principia,* i. 35.

transcendent act of will in which truth and good had their origin.

The inherent defect of this view is the divorce it makes between the form and the matter of intelligence. It implies that reason or self-consciousness is one thing, and that truth is another and quite different thing, which has been united to it by the arbitrary will of God. The same external conception of the relation of truth to the mind is involved in the doctrine of innate ideas. It is true that Des Cartes did not hold that doctrine in the coarse form in which it was attributed to him by Locke, but expressly declares that he has "never said or thought at any time that the mind required innate ideas which were separated from the faculty of thinking. He had simply used the word innate to distinguish those ideas which are derived from that faculty, and not from external objects or the determination of the will. Just as when we say generosity is innate in certain families, and in certain other diseases, like the gout or the stone, we do not mean to imply that infants in their mother's womb are affected with these complaints."[1] Yet Des Cartes, as we have

[1] *Notæ in Programma*, 184.

seen, does not hold that these truths are involved in the very nature of intelligence as such, so that we cannot conceive a self-conscious being without them. On the contrary, we are to regard the divine intelligence as by arbitrary act determining that two and two should be four, or that envy should be a vice. We are "*not* to conceive eternal truth flowing from God as rays from the sun."[1] In other words, we are not to conceive all particular truths as different aspects of one truth. It is part of the imperfection of man's finite nature that he "finds truth and good determined for him." It is something given,—given, indeed, along with his very faculty of thinking,—but still *given* as an external limit to it. It belongs not to his nature as spirit, but to his finitude as man.

After what has been said, it is obvious that the transition from God to matter must be somewhat arbitrary and external. God's truthfulness is pledged for the reality of that of which we have clear and distinct ideas; and we have clear and distinct ideas of the external world so long as we conceive it simply as extended matter, infinitely

[1] *Epistolæ*, i. 110.

divisible, and moved entirely from without,—so long, in short, as we conceive it as the direct opposite of mind, and do not attribute to it any one of the properties of mind. *Omnes proprietates, quas in ea clare percipimus, ad hoc unum reducuntur, quod sit partibilis et mobilis secundum partes.* We must, therefore, free ourselves from the obscure and confused modes of thought which arise whenever we attribute any of the secondary qualities, which exist merely in our sensations, to the objects that cause these sensations. The subjective character of such qualities is proved by the constant change which takes place in them, without any change of the object in which they are perceived. A piece of wax cannot lose its extension; but its colour, its hardness, and all the other qualities whereby it is presented to sense may be easily altered. What is objective in all this is merely an extended substance, and the modes of motion or rest through which it is made to pass. In like manner we must separate from our notion of matter all ideas of *actio in distans: e.g.*, we must explain weight not as a tendency to the centre of the earth or an attraction of distant particles of matter, but as a consequence of the pressure of other bodies, immediately surrounding that which is felt to be heavy.[1] For the only conceivable *actio in distans* is that which is mediated by thought, and it is only in so far as we suppose matter to have in it a principle of activity like thought that we can accept such explanations of its motion. Again, while we must thus keep our conception of matter clear of all elements that do not belong to it, we must also be careful not to take away from it those that *do* belong to it. It is a defect of distinctness in our ideas when we conceive an attribute as existing apart from its substance, or a substance without its attribute; for this is to treat elements that are only separated by a "distinction of reason," as if they were distinct things. The conception of the possibility of a vacuum or empty space arises merely from our confusing the possible separation of any particular mode or form of matter from matter in general, with the impossible separation of matter in general from its own essential attribute. Accordingly, in his physical philosophy, Des Cartes attempts to explain everything on mechanical principles, starting with the hypothesis that a certain quantity of motion has been communicated to the material universe

[1] *Resp. Sextæ*, 165-6.

by God at the first, a quantity which can never be lost or diminished, and that space is an absolute plenum in which motion propagates itself in circles. It is unnecessary to follow Des Cartes into the detail of the theory of vortices. It is more to the purpose to notice the nature of the reasons by which he is driven to regard such a mechanical explanation of the universe as necessary. A real or substantive existence is, in his view, a *res completa*, a thing that can be conceived as a whole in itself without relations to any other thing. Now matter and mind are, he thinks, such complete existences, so long as we conceive them, as the pure intelligence must conceive them, as abstract opposites of each other; and do not permit ourselves to be confused by those mixed modes of thought which are due to sense or imagination. Des Cartes does not see that in this very abstract opposition there is a bond of union between mind and matter, or, in other words, that they are correlative opposites, and therefore in their separation *res incompletæ*. In other words, they are merely elements of reality substantiated by abstract thought into independent realities. He indeed partly retracts his assertion that mind and matter severed from each other are *res completæ*, when he declares that neither can be conceived as existing apart from God, and that therefore, strictly speaking, God alone is a substance. But as we have seen, he avoids the necessary inference that in God the opposition between mind and matter is reconciled or transcended, by conceiving God as abstract self-consciousness or will, and the material world not as His necessary manifestation, but simply as His creation, *i.e.*, as having its origin in an act of bare volition, and that only. His God is the God of abstract Monotheism and not of Christianity, and in relation to such a God, the world must be conceived as a foreign matter which He brings into being, and acts on from without, but in which He is not revealed.

It is a natural consequence of this view that nature is essentially *dead matter*, and that beyond the motion it has received from God at the beginning, and which it transmits from part to part without increase or diminution, it has in itself no principle of activity. Every trace of vitality in it must be explained away as a mere false reflection upon it of the nature of mind. The world is thus " cut in two with a hatchet," and there is no attraction to overcome the mutual repulsion of its severed parts. Nothing can be admitted in the material half that savours of self determination, all its energy must be communicated, not self-originated; there is in it no room for gravitation, still less for magnetism or chemical affinity. *A fortiori*, animal life must be completely explained away. The machine may be very complicated, but it is still, and can be nothing but a machine. For if we once admitted that matter could be anything but mechanical, we should be on the way to admit that matter could become mind. When a modern physical philosopher declares that everything, even life and thought, is ultimately reducible to matter, we cannot always be certain that he means what he seems to say. Not seldom the materialist *soi-disant*, when we hear his account of the properties of matter, turns out to be something like a spiritualist in disguise; but when Des Cartes asserted that everything *but* mind is material, and that the animals are automata, there is no such dubiety of interpretation. He said what he meant, and meant what he said, in the hardest sense his words can bear. *His* matter was not even gravitating, much less living; it had no property except that of retaining and transmitting the motion received from without by pressure and impact. And *his* animals were automata, not merely in the sense of being governed by sensation and instinct, but precisely in the sense that a watch is an automaton. Henry More cries out against the ruthless consequence with which he develops his principles to this result. " In this," he says, " I do not so much admire the penetrative power of your genius as I tremble for the fate of the animals. What I recognise in you is not only subtlety of thought, but a hard and remorseless logic with which you arm yourself as with a sword of steel, to take away life and sensation with one blow, from almost the whole animal kingdom." But Des Cartes was not the man to be turned from the legitimate result of his principles by a scream. " Nec moror astutias et sagacitates canum et vulpium, nec quæcunque alia propter cibum, venerem, aut metum a brutis fiunt. *Profiteor enim me posse perfacile illa omnia ut a sola membrorum conformatione profecta explicare.*"[1]

The difficulty reaches its height when Des Cartes

---

[1] *Epist.* i. 66, 67. Cf., however, the passages quoted by Mr. Martineau (*Types of Ethical Theory*, II. 138) which show that Des Cartes sometimes made concessions in relation to the sensitive life of animals similar to those which, as we shall immediately see, he makes in relation to the sensitive life of man, see especially *Œuvres*, ix. 423-53; x. 207 -8.

attempts to explain the union of the body and spirit in man. Between two substances which, when clearly and distinctly conceived, do not imply each other, there can be none but an artificial unity, —a unity of composition that still leaves them external to each other. Even God cannot make them one in any higher sense.[2] And as it is impossible in the nature of mind to see any reason why it should be embodied, or in the nature of matter to see any reason why it should become the organ of mind, the union of the two must be taken as a mere empirical fact. When we put on the one side all that belongs to intelligence, and on the other all that belongs to matter, there is a residuum in our ideas which we cannot reduce to either head. This residuum consists of our appetites, our passions, and our sensations, including not only the feelings of pain and pleasure, but also the perceptions of colour, smell, taste, of hardness and softness, and all the other qualities apprehended by touch. These must be referred to the union of mind with body. They are subjective in the sense that they give us no information either as to the nature of things or of mind. Their function is only to indicate what

[2] *Princ.* i. 60.

things are useful or hurtful to our composite nature as such, or, in other words, what things tend to confirm or dissolve the unity of mind and body. They indicate that *something* is taking place in our body or without it, and so stimulate us to some kind of action, but *what* it is that is taking place they do not tell us. There is no resemblance in the sensation of pain produced by great heat to the tension of the fibres of our body that causes it. But we do not need to know the real origin of our sensation to prevent us going too near the fire. Sensation leads us into error only when we are not conscious that its office is merely practical, and when we attempt to make objective judgments by means of its obscure and confused ideas, *e.g.*, when we say that there is heat in our hands or in the fire. And the remedy for this error is to be found simply in the clear conviction of the subjectivity of sensation.

These views of the nature of sense, however, at once force us to ask how Des Cartes can consistently admit that a subjective result such as sensation, a result in mind, should be produced by matter, and on the other hand how an objective result, a result in matter, should be effected by mind. Des Cartes explains at great length, according to his modification of the physiology of the day, that the pineal gland, which is the immediate organ of the soul, is acted on by the nerves through the "animal spirits," and again by reaction upon these spirits produces motions in the body. It is an obvious remark that this explanation either materialises mind, or else puts for the solution the very problem to be solved. It was therefore in the spirit of Des Cartes, it was only making explicit what is involved in many of his expressions, when Geulincx, one of his earliest followers, formulated the theory of occasional causes. The general approval of the Cartesian school showed that this was a legitimate development of doctrine. Yet it tore away the last veil from the absolute dualism of the system, which had stretched the antagonism of mind and matter so far that no mediation remained possible, or, what is the same thing, so far that it remained possible only through an inexplicable will of God. The intrusion of such a *Deus ex machina* into philosophy only showed that by its violent abstraction philosophy had destroyed the unity of the known and intelligible world, and was, therefore, forced to seek that unity in the region of the unknown and unintelligible. If our light be darkness, then in our darkness we must seek for light; if reason be contradictory in itself, truth must be found in unreason. The development of the Cartesian school was soon to show what is the necessary and inevitable consequence of such worship of the unknown.

To the ethical aspect of his philosophy, Des Cartes, unlike his great disciple, only devoted a subordinate attention. In a short treatise, however, he discussed the relation of reason to the passions. After we have got over the initial difficulty, that matter should give rise to effects in mind, and mind in matter, and have admitted that in man the unity of mind and body turns what in the animals is mere mechanical reception of stimulus from without and reaction upon it, into an action and reaction mediated by sensation, emotion, and passion, another question presents itself. How can the mere natural movement of passion, the nature of which is fixed by the original constitution of our body and of the things that act upon it, be altered or modified by pure reason? For while it is obvious that morality consists in the determination of reason by itself, it is not easy to conceive how the same being who is determined by passion from without should also be determined by reason from within. How, in other words, can a spiritual being maintain its character as self-determined, or at least determined only by the clear and distinct ideas of the reason which are its innate forms, in the presence of this foreign element of passion that seems to make it the slave of external impressions? Is reason able to crush this intruder, or to turn it into a servant? Can the passions be annihilated, or can they be spiritualised?

Des Cartes could not properly adopt either alternative; he could not adopt the ethics of asceticism, for the union of body and mind is, in his view, natural; and hence the passions which are the results of that union are in themselves relatively good. They are provisions of nature for the protection of the unity of soul and body, and stimulate us to the acts necessary for that purpose. Yet, on the other hand, he could not admit that these passions are capable of being completely spiritualised; for so long as the unity of body and soul is regarded as merely external and accidental, it is impossible to think that the passions which arise out of this unity can be transformed into the embodiment and expression of reason. Des Cartes, indeed, points out that every passion has a lower and a higher form, and while in its lower or primary form it is based on the obscure ideas produced by the motion of the animal spirits, in its higher form it is connected with the clear and distinct judgments of reason regarding good and evil. If, however, the unity of soul and body be a unity of composition, there is an element of obscurity in the judgments of passion which cannot be made clear, an element in desire which cannot be spiritualised. If the mind be external to the passions, it can only impose upon them an external rule of moderation. On such a theory no *ideal* morality is possible to man in his present state; for, in order to the attainment of such an ideal morality, it would be necessary that the accidental element, which is obtruded into his life as a spiritual being by his connection with the body, should be expelled. What can be attained under present conditions is only, to abstract so far as is possible from external things, and from those relations to external things into which passion brings us. Hence the great importance which Des Cartes attaches to the distinction between things in our power, and things not in our power. What is not in our power includes all outward things, and therefore it is our highest wisdom to regard them as determined by an absolute fate or the eternal decree of God. We cease to wish for that which is seen to be impossible ; and therefore, in order to subdue our passions we only need to convince ourselves that no effort of ours can enable us to secure their objects. On the other hand, that which is within our power, and which therefore we cannot desire too earnestly, is virtue. But virtue in this abstraction from all objects of desire is simply the harmony of reason with itself, the $\dot{a}\tau a\rho a\xi i a$ of the Stoic under a slight change of aspect. Thus in ethics, as in metaphysics, Des Cartes ends not with a reconciliation of the opposed elements, but with a dualism, or, at best, with a unity which is the result of abstraction.

MALEBRANCHE was prepared, by the ascetic training of the cloister and the teaching of Augustine, to bring to clear consciousness and expression many of the tendencies that were latent and undeveloped in the philosophy of Des Cartes. To use a chemical metaphor, the Christian Platonism of the church father was a medium in which Cartesianism could precipitate the product of its elements. Yet the medium was, as we shall see, not a perfect one, and hence the product was not quite pure. Without metaphor, Malebranche, by his previous habits of thought, was well fitted to detect and develop the pantheistic and ascetic elements of his master's philosophy. But he was not well fitted to penetrate through the veil of popular language under which the discordance of that philosophy with orthodox Christianity was hidden. On the contrary, the whole training of the Catholic priest, and especially his practical spirit, with that tendency to compromise which a practical spirit always brings with it, enabled him to conceal from himself as well as from others the logical result of his principles. And we do not wonder even when we find him treating as a " wretched creature" (*miserable*) the philosopher who tore away the veil.

Malebranche "*saw all things in God.*" In other words, he taught that knowledge is possible only in so far as thought is the expression, not of the nature of the individual subject as such, but of a universal life in which he and all other rational beings partake. "No one can feel my individual pain ; every one can see the truth which I contemplate—why is it so ? The reason is that my pain is a modification of my substance, but truth is the common good of all spirits."[1] This idea is ever present to Malebranche, and is repeated by him in an endless variety of forms of expression. Thus, like Des Cartes, but with more decision, he tells us that the idea of the infinite is prior to the idea of the finite. "We conceive of the infinite being by the very fact that we conceive of 'being,' without considering whether it be finite or no. But in order that we may think of a finite being, we must necessarily cut off or deduct something from the general notion of being, which consequently we must previously possess. Thus the mind does not apprehend anything whatever, except in and through the idea that it has of the infinite; nor is it the case that, as philosophers have maintained, this idea is formed by the confused assemblage of all the ideas of particular things. On the contrary, all these particular ideas are only participations in the general idea of the infinite, just as God does not derive His being from the creatures, but all the creatures are imperfect participations of the Divine Being."[2] Again, he tells us, in the same chapter, that "when we wish to think of any particular thing, we first cast our view

[1] *Morale*, i. 1, § 2.   [2] *Recherche*, III. ii. 6.

upon all being, and then apply it to the consideration of the object in question. We could not desire to see any particular object, unless we saw it already in a confused and general way, and as there is nothing which we cannot desire to see, so all objects must be in a manner present to our spirit." Or, as he puts it in another place, " our mind would not be capable of representing to itself the general ideas of genera and species, if it did not see all things as contained in one; for, every creature being an individual, we cannot say that we are apprehending any created thing when we think the general idea of a triangle !"

The main idea that is expressed in all these different ways is simply this, that to determine any individual object as such, we must relate it to, and distinguish it from, the whole of which it is a part; and that, therefore, thought could never apprehend anything, if it did not bring with itself the idea of the intelligible world as a unity. Des Cartes had already expressed this truth in his *Meditations*, but he had deprived it of its full significance by making a distinction between the *being* and the *idea* of God, the former of which, in his view, was only the cause of the latter. Malebranche detects this error, and denies that there is any idea of the infinite, which is a somewhat crude way of saying that there is no division between the idea of the infinite and its reality. What Reid asserted of the external world, that it is not represented by an idea in our minds, but is actually present to them, Malebranche asserted of God. No individual thing, he tells us—and an idea is but an individual thing—could represent the infinite. On the contrary, all individual things are represented through the infinite Being, who contains them all in His substance *très efficace, et par conséquence très intelligible*.[1] We know God by Himself, material things only by their ideas in God, for they are "unintelligible in themselves, and we can see them only in the being who contains them in an intelligible manner." And thus, unless we in some way "saw God, we should be able to see nothing else." The vision *of* God or *in* God, therefore, is an "intellectual intuition," in which seer and seen, knower and known, are one. Our knowledge of things is our participation in God's knowledge of them. When we have gone so far with Malebranche, we are tempted to ask why he does not follow out his thought to its natural conclusion.

[1] *Recherche*, III. ii. 6, 7.

If the idea of God is not separable from His existence, if it is through the idea of Him that all things are known, and through His existence that all things are, then it would seem necessarily to follow that our consciousness of God is but a part of God's consciousness of Himself, that our consciousness of self and other things is but God's consciousness of them, and lastly, that there is no existence either of ourselves or other things except in this consciousness. To understand Malebranche is mainly to understand how he stopped short of results that seemed to lie so directly in the line of his thought.

To begin with the last point, it is easy to see that Malebranche only asserts unity of idea and reality in God, in order to deny it everywhere else; which with him is equivalent to asserting it in general and denying it in particular. To him, as to Des Cartes, the opposition between mind and matter is absolute. Material things cannot come into our minds, nor can our minds go out of themselves *pour se promener dans les cieux*.[1] Hence they are in themselves absolutely unknown; they are known only in God, in whom are their ideas;

[1] *Recherche*, III. ii. 1.

and as these ideas are quite distinct from the reality, they "might be presented to the mind without anything existing." That they exist *out of* God in another manner than the intelligible manner of their existence *in* God, is explained by a mere act of His will, that is, it is not explained at all. Though we see all things in God, therefore, there is no connection between His existence and theirs. The "world is not a necessary emanation of divinity; God is perfectly self-sufficient, and the idea of the infinitely perfect Being can be conceived quite apart from any other. The existence of the creatures is due to the free decrees of God."[1] Malebranche, therefore, still treats of external things as "things in themselves," which have an existence apart from thought, even the divine thought, though it is only in and through the divine thought they can be known by us. "To see the material world, or rather to judge that it exists (since in itself it is invisible), it is necessary that God should reveal it to us, for we cannot see the result of His arbitrary will through necessary reason."[2]

But if we know external things only through their idea in God, how do we know ourselves? Is

[1] *Morale*, I. i. § 5.   [2] *Entretien*, I. § 5.

it also through the idea of us in God? Here we come upon a point in which Malebranche diverges very far from his master. We do not, he says, properly *know* ourselves at all, as we know God, or even external objects. We are conscious of ourselves by inner sense (*sentiment intérieur*), and from this we know *that* we are, but we do not know *what* we are. "We know the existence of our soul more distinctly than of our body, but we have not so perfect a knowledge of our soul as of our body." This is shown by the fact that from our idea of body as extended substance, we can, at once see what are its possible modifications. In other words, we only need the idea of extended substance to see that there is an inexhaustible number of figures and motions of which it is capable. The whole of geometry is but a development of what is given already in the conception of extension. But it is not so with our consciousness of self, which does not enable us to say, prior to actual experience, what sensations or passions are possible to us. We only know what heat, cold, light, colour, hunger, anger, and desire are by feeling them. Our knowledge extends as far as our experience and no further. Nay, we have good reason to believe that many of these modifications exist in our soul only by reason of its accidental association with a body, and that, if it were freed from that body, it would be capable of far other and higher experiences. "We know by feeling that our soul is great, but perhaps we know almost nothing of what it is in itself." The information which sense gives has, as Des Cartes taught, only a practical but no theoretical value; it tells us nothing of the external world, the real nature of which we know, not through touch and taste and sight, but only through our idea of extended substance; while of the nature of the soul it does not tell us much more than that it exists, and that it is not material. And in this latter case we have no idea, nothing better than sense to raise us above its illusions.

It is clear from these statements that by self-consciousness Malebranche means consciousness of desires and feelings, which belong to the individual as such, and not consciousness of the self as thinking. He begins, in fact, where Des Cartes ended, and identifies the consciousness of self as thinking, and so transcending the limits of its own particular being, with the consciousness or idea of God. And between the consciousness of the finite in sense, and the consciousness of the infinite in thought, or in other words, between the consciousness of the universal and the consciousness of the individual, he sees no connection. Malebranche is just one step from the pantheistic conclusion that the consciousness of finite individuality as such is illusory, and that as all bodies are but modes of one infinite extension, so all souls are but modes of one infinite thought. But while he willingly accepts this result in regard to matter, his religious feelings prevent him from accepting it in relation to mind. He is driven, therefore, to the inconsistency of holding that sense and feeling, through which in his view we apprehend the finite as such, give us true though imperfect knowledge of the soul, while the knowledge they give us of body is not only imperfect but false.[1] Thus the finite spirit is still allowed to be a substance, distinct from the infinite, though it holds its substantial existence on a precarious tenure. It is left hanging, we may say, on the verge of the infinite, whose attraction must soon prove too strong for it. Ideas are living things, and often remould the minds that admit them in spite of the greatest resistance of dead custom and

[1] *Recherche*, III. ii. 7, § 4.

traditionary belief. In the grasp of a logic that overpowers him, the more easily that he is unconscious of its tendency, Malebranche is brought within one step of the pantheistic conclusion, and all that his Christian feeling and priestly training can do, is *just* to save him from the denial of the personality of man.

But even this denial is not the last word of pantheism. When the principle that the finite is known only in relation to the infinite, the individual only in relation to the universal, is interpreted as meaning that the infinite and universal is complete in itself without the finite and individual, and when the finite and individual is treated as a mere accidental existence due to the "arbitrary will of God," it ceases to be possible to conceive even God as a spirit. Did Malebranche realise what he was saying when he declared that God was "being in general," but not any particular being? At any rate we can see that the same logic which leads him almost to deny the reality of finite beings, leads him also to seek the divine nature in something more abstract and general even than thought. If we must abstract from all relation to the finite in order to know God as He is, is it not necessary for us also to abstract from self-consciousness? For self-consciousness also has a negative element in it; it is something definite and therefore limited. We do not wonder, therefore, when we find Malebranche saying that reason does not tell us that God is a spirit, but only that He is an infinitely perfect being. He is conceived as a spirit rather than as a body only, because spirit is more perfect than body. "When we call God a spirit, it is not so much to show positively what He is, as to signify that He is not material." But as we ought not to give Him a bodily form like man's, so we ought not to think of His spirit as similar to our own spirits, although we can conceive nothing more perfect. "It is necessary rather to believe that as He contains in Himself the properties of matter without being material, so He comprehends in Himself the perfections of created spirits without being like any spirit we can conceive, and that His true name is "He who is," *i.e.*, Being without restriction, Being infinite and universal."[1] .

Thus the essentially self-revealing God of Christianity gives way to pure spirit, and pure spirit in its turn to the eternal and incomprehensible sub-

[1] *Recherche*, III. ii. 9.

stance, of which we can say nothing but that it is. The divine substance contains in itself, indeed, all the elements that are in creation, but it contains them *eminenter*, in some incomprehensible form that is reconcilable with its infinitude. But we have no adequate name by which to call it except Being. The curious metaphysic of theology by which, in his later writings, Malebranche tried to make room for the incarnation, by supposing that the finite creation, which *as* finite is unworthy of God, was made worthy by union with Christ, the divine Word, shows that Malebranche had some indistinct sense of the necessity of reconciling his philosophy with his theology; but it shows also the necessarily artificial nature of the combination. The result of the union of such incongruous elements was something which the theologians at once recognised as heterodox, and the philosophers as illogical.

There was another doctrine of Malebranche which brought him into trouble with the theologians, and which was the main subject of his long controversy with Arnauld. This was his denial of particular providence. As Leibniz maintained that this is the best of all possible worlds, and that its evils are to be explained by the negative nature of the finite, so Malebranche, with a slight difference of expression, derived evil from the nature of particular or individual existence. It is not conformable to the nature of God to act by any but universal laws, and these universal laws necessarily involve particular evil consequences, though their ultimate result is the highest possible good. The question why there should be any particular existence, any existence *but* God, seeing such existence necessarily involves evil, remains insoluble so long as the purely pantheistic view of God is maintained; and it is this view which is really at the bottom of the assertion that He can have no particular volitions. To the coarse and anthropomorphic conception of particular providence Malebranche may be right in objecting; but, on the other hand, it cannot be doubted that any theory in which the universal is absolutely opposed to the particular, the infinite to the finite, is unchristian as well as unphilosophical. For under this dualistic presupposition, there seem to be only two possible alternatives open to thought; *either* the particular and finite must be treated as something independent of the universal and infinite, ✦ which involves an obvious contradiction, *or* else it must be regarded as absolute nonentity. We find

Malebranche doing the one or the other as occasion requires. Thus he vindicates the freedom of man's will on the ground that the universal will of God does not completely determine the particular volitions of man; and then, becoming conscious of the difficulty involved in this conception, he tries, like Des Cartes, to explain the particular will as something merely negative, a defect, and not a positive existence.

But to understand fully Malebranche's view of freedom and the ethical system connected with it, we must notice an important alteration which he makes in the Cartesian theory of the relation of will and intelligence. To Des Cartes, as we have seen, the ultimate essence of mind lay in pure abstract self-determination or will, and hence he based even moral and intellectual truth on the arbitrary decrees of God. With Malebranche, abstraction goes a step further; and the absolute is sought, not in the subject as opposed to the object, not in pure formal self-determination as opposed to that which is determined, but in a unity that transcends this difference. With him, therefore, will ceases to be regarded as the essence of intelligence, and sinks into a property or separable attribute of it. As we can conceive an extended substance without actual movement, so, he says, we can conceive a thinking substance without actual volition. But "matter or extension without motion would be entirely useless and incapable of that variety of forms for which it is made; and we cannot, therefore, suppose, that an all-wise Being would create it in this way. In like manner, if a spiritual or thinking substance were without will, it is clear that it would be quite useless, for it would not be attracted towards the objects of its perception, and would not love the good for which it is made. We cannot therefore conceive an intelligent being so to fashion it."[1] Now God need not be conceived as creating at all, for He is self-sufficient; but if He be a creator of spirits, He must create them for Himself. "God cannot will that there should exist a spirit that does not love Him, or that loves Him less than any other good."[2] The craving for good in general, for an absolute satisfaction, is a *natural* love of God that is common to all. "The just, the wicked, the blessed, and the damned all alike love God with this love." Out of this love of God arises the love we have to ourselves and to

---

[1] *Recherche*, I. i. 1. [2] *Ibid.* I. i. 4.

others, which are the *natural inclinations* that belong to all created spirits. For these inclinations are but the elements of the love which is in God, and which therefore he inspires in all his creatures. "*Il s'aime, il nous aime, il aime toutes ses créatures; il ne fait donc point d'esprits qu'il ne les porte à l'aimer, à s'aimer, et à aimer toutes les créatures.*"[1] Stripping this thought of its theological vesture, what is expressed here is simply that, as a spiritual being, each man is conscious of his own limited and individual existence, as well as of the limited and individual existence of other beings like himself, only in relation to the whole in which they are parts. Hence he can find his own good only in the good of the whole, and he is in contradiction with himself so long as he rests in any good short of that. His love of happiness, his natural inclinations both selfish and social, may be therefore regarded as an undeveloped form of the love of God; and the ideal state of his inclinations is that in which the love of self and of others are explicitly referred to that higher affection; or in which his love does not proceed from a part to the whole, but from the whole to the parts.

[1] *Recherche*, I. iv. 1.

The question of morals to Malebranche is the question how these *natural inclinations* are related to the particular passions. Sensation and passion arise out of the connection of body and soul, and their use is only to urge us to attend to the wants of the former. We can scarcely hear without a smile the simple monastic legend which Malebranche weaves together about the original nature of the passions and their alteration by the Fall. "It is a manifest indication of disorder that a spirit, capable of knowing and loving God, should be obliged to occupy itself with the needs of the body." "A being altogether occupied with what passes in his body and with the infinity of objects that surround it, cannot be thinking on the things that are truly good."[1] Hence the necessity of an immediate and instinctive warning from the senses in regard to the relations of things to our organism, and also of pains and pleasures which may induce us to attend to this warning. "Sensible pleasure is the mark that nature has attached to the use of certain things in order that, without having the trouble of examining them by reason, we may employ them for the preservation of the body, but not in order that we may

[1] *Entretien,* iv.

love them."[1] Till the Fall the mind was merely united to the body, not subjected to it, and the influence of these pleasures and pains was only such as to make men attend to their bodily wants, but not to occupy the mind, or fill it with sensuous joys and sorrows, or trouble its contemplation of that which is really good. Our moral aim should therefore be to restore this state of things, to weaken our union with the body and strengthen our union with God. And to encourage us in pursuing this aim we have to remember that union with God is natural to the spirit, and that, while even the condition of union with the body is artificial, the condition of subjection to the body is wholly unnatural to it. Our primary tendency is towards the supreme good, and we love the objects of our passions only in so far as we "determine towards particular, and therefore false goods, the love that God gives us for himself." The search for happiness is really the search for God in disguise, and even the levity and inconstancy with which men rush from one finite good to another, is a proof that they were made for the infinite. Furthermore, this natural love of God, or inclination for good in general, "gives us the power

[1] *Recherche*, v. 4.

of suspending our consent in regard to those particular goods which do not satisfy it."[1] If we refuse to be led by the obscure and confused voice of instinctive feeling, which arises from and always tends to confirm our union with the body, and if we wait for the light of reason which arises from our union with God, and always tends to confirm it, we are doing all that is in our power, and the rest must be left to God. "If we only judge precisely of that which we see clearly, we shall never be deceived. For then it will not be we that judge, but the universal reason that judges in us."[2] And as our love, even of particular goods, is a confused love of the supreme good, so the clear vision of God inevitably brings with it the love of Him. "We needs must love the highest when we see it." When it is the divine reason that speaks in us, it is the divine love that moves us, "the same love wherewith God loves Himself and the things He has made."[3]

The general result of the ethics of Malebranche is ascetic. The passions, like the senses, have no relation to the higher life of the soul; their value is only in relation to the union of soul and body, a

---

[1] *Recherche*, iv. 1.   [2] *Morale*, I. i. § 9.
[3] *Recherche*, iv. 5.

union which is purely accidental or due to the arbitrary will of God. As Pericles said of women that the less they were heard of in public for good or evil the better, so Malebranche would say of the sensations and passions, that the more silently they discharge their provisional function, and the less they disturb or interfere with the pure activity of spirit, the more nearly they approach to the only perfection that is possible for them. Their ideal state is to remain or become again simple instincts that act mechanically like the circulation of the blood. The universal light of reason casts no ray into the obscurity of sense; its universal love cannot embrace any of the objects of particular passion. It is indeed recognised by Malebranche that sensation in man is mixed with thought, that the passions in him are forms of the love of good in general. But this union of the rational with the sensuous nature is regarded merely as a confusion which is to be cleared up, *not* in a higher unity of the two elements, but simply by the withdrawal of the spirit from contact with that which darkens and defiles it. Of a transformation of sense into thought, of passion into duty,—an elevation of the life of sense which turns it into the embodiment and expression of the life of reason,—Malebranche has no conception.

Hence the life of reason turns with him to mysticism in theory and to asceticism in practice. His universal is abstract and opposed to the particular; instead of explaining, it explains it away. A certain tender beauty as of twilight is spread over the world as we view it through the eyes of this cloistered philosopher, and we do not at first see that the softness and ideality of the picture is due to the gathering darkness. Abstraction seems only to be purifying and not destroying, till it has done its perfect work. Malebranche conceived himself to be presenting to the world only the purest and most refined expression of Christian ethics and theology. But if we obey his own continual advice to think clearly and distinctly, if we divest his system of all the sensuous and imaginative forms in which he has clothed it, and reduce it to the naked simplicity of its central thought, what we find is not a God that reveals Himself in the finite and to the finite, but an absolute Substance which has no revelation, and whose existence is the negation of all but itself. To tear away the veil, however, there was needed a stronger, simpler, and freer spirit,—a spirit less influenced by opinion, less inclined to practical compromise, and gifted with a stronger "faith in the whispers of the lonely muse" of speculation, than Malebranche.

It is a remark of Hegel's that SPINOZA, as a Jew, first brought into European thought the idea of an absolute unity in which the difference of finite and infinite is lost. Some later writers have gone further, and attempted to show that the main doctrines by which his philosophy is distinguished from that of Des Cartes were due to the direct influences of Jewish writers like Maimonides, and Chasdai Creskas, rather than to the necessary development of Cartesian ideas. And it is undoubtedly true that many points of similarity with such writers, reaching down even to verbal coincidence, may be detected in the works of Spinoza, although it is not so easy to determine how much he owed to their teaching. His own view of his obligations is sufficiently indicated by the fact that, while in his ethics he carries on a continual polemic against Des Cartes, and strives at every point to show that his own doctrines are legitimately derived from Cartesian principles, he only once refers to Jewish philosophy as containing an obscure and unreasoned anticipation of these doctrines." "*Quod quidam Hebræorum quasi per nebulam vidisse videntur, qui scilicet statuunt Deum Dei intellectum resque ab ipso intellectas unum et idem esse.*"[1] It may be that the undeveloped pantheism and rationalism of the Jewish philosophers had a deeper influence upon Spinoza than he himself was aware of, particularly in emancipating him from the traditions of the synagogue, and giving to his mind its first philosophical bias. In his earlier work, *De Deo et Homini*, there are Neo-Platonic ideas and expressions, which in the *Ethics* are rejected or remoulded into a form more suitable to the spirit of Cartesianism. But the question, after all, has little more than a biographical interest. In the Spinozistic philosophy there are few differences from Des Cartes which cannot be traced to the necessary development of Cartesian principles; and the case of Malebranche shows that the development might take place under the most diverse intellectual conditions. What is most remarkable in Spinoza is just the freedom and security with which these principles are followed out to their last result. His

[1] *Eth.* ii. Prop. 7.

Jewish origin and his breach with Judaism completely isolated him from every influence but that of the thought that possessed him. And no scruple or hesitation, no respect for the institutions or feelings of his time, interfered with the speculative development of his principles. He exhibits to us the almost perfect type of a mind without superstitions, which has freed itself from all but reasoned and intelligent convictions, or, in the Cartesian phrase, "clear and distinct ideas"; and when he fails, it is not by any inconsistency, or abitrary stopping short of the necessary conclusions of his logic, but by the essential defect of his principles.

Spinoza takes his idea of method from mathematics, and after the manner of Euclid, places at the head of each book of his *Ethics* a certain number of definitions, axioms, and postulates, which are supposed to be intuitively certain, and to form a sufficient basis for all that follows. Altogether there are twenty-seven definitions, twenty axioms, and eight postulates. If Spinoza is regarded as the most consequent of philosophers, it cannot be because he has based his system upon so many fragmentary views of truth; it must be because a deeper unity has been discerned in the system than is visible on the first aspect of it. We must, therefore, to a certain extent distinguish between the form and the matter of his thought, though it is also true that the defective form itself involves a defect in the matter.

What in the first instance recommends the geometrical method to Spinoza is, not only its apparent exactness and the necessity of its sequence, but, so to speak, its disinterestedness. Confusion of thought arises from the fact that we put ourselves, our desires and feelings and interests, into our view of things; that we do not regard them as they are in themselves in their essential nature, but look for some final cause, that is, for some relation to ourselves, by which they may be explained. For this reason, he says, "the truth might for ever have remained hid from the human race, if mathematics, which looks not to the final cause of figures, but to their essential nature and the properties involved in it, had not set another type of knowledge before them." To understand things is to see how all that is true of them flows from the clear and distinct idea expressed in their definition, and ultimately, it is to see how all truth flows from the *essentia Dei*, just as geometrical truth flows from the idea of space. To take a mathematical view of the universe, therefore, is to raise ourselves above all consideration of the end or tendency of things, above the fears and hopes of mortality, into the region of truth and necessity. "When I turned my mind to this subject," he says in the beginning of his treatise on Politics, "I did not propose to myself any novel or strange aim, but simply to demonstrate by certain and indubitable reason those things which agree best with practice. And in order that I might inquire into the matters of this science with the same freedom of mind with which we are wont to treat lines and surfaces in mathematics, I determined not to laugh or to weep over the actions of men, but simply to understand them; and to contemplate their affections and passions, such as love, hate, anger, envy, arrogance, pity, and all other disturbances of soul, not as vices of human nature, but as properties pertaining to it, in the same way as heat, cold, storm, thunder pertain to the nature of the atmosphere. For these, though troublesome, are yet necessary, and have certain causes through which we may come to understand them, and thus, by contemplating them in their truth, gain for our minds as much joy as by the knowledge of things that are pleasing to the senses." All our errors as to the nature of things arise from our judging them from the point of view of the part and not of the whole, from a point of view determined by their relation to our own individual being, and not from a point of view determined by the nature of the things themselves; or, to put the same thing in another way, from the point of view of sense and imagination, and not from the point of view of intelligence. The science of mathematics shows us the inadequacy of such knowledge, when it takes us out of ourselves into things, and when it presents these things to us as objects of universal intelligence apart from all special relation to our individual feelings. And Spinoza only wishes that the same universality and freedom of thought, which belongs to mathematics, because its objects *do not* interest the passions, should be extended to those objects that *do* interest them. The first condition of the philosopher's being is to free his mind from subjective interests, and to get beyond the illusion of sense and passion, which makes our own lives so supremely important and interesting to us simply because they are our own. He must look at what is immediately present to him as it were through an inverted telescope of reason, which reduces it to its due proportion and place in the sum of things. To the heat of passion and the higher heat of imagination, Spinoza has only one advice: " Acquaint yourself with God and be at peace. Look not to the particular but to the universal, view things not under the form of the finite and temporal, but *sub quadam specie æternitatis.*"

The illusion of the finite, the illusion of sense, imagination, and passion,—which, in Bacon's language, tends to make men judge of things *ex analogia hominis* and not *ex analogia universi*, which raises the individual life, and even the present moment of the individual life with its passing feelings, into a standard for measuring the universe,—this, in the eyes of Spinoza, is the source of all error and evil to man. On the other hand, his highest good is to live the universal life of reason, or, what is the same thing, to view all things from their centre in God, and to be moved only by the passion for good in general, "the intellectual love of God." In the treatise *De Emendatione Intellectus*, Spinoza takes up this contrast in the first instance from its moral side. "All our felicity or infelicity is founded on the nature of the object to which we are joined by love." To love the things that perish is to be in continual trouble and disturbance of passion; it is to be full of envy and hatred towards others who possess them: it is to be ever striving after that which, when we attain it, does not satisfy us; or lamenting over the loss of that which inevitably passes away from us; only "love to an object which is infinite and eternal feeds the soul with a changeless and unmingled joy." But, again, our love rests upon our knowledge; if we saw things as they really are, we should love only the highest object. It is because sense and imagination give to the finite an independence and substantiality that do not belong to it, that we waste our love upon it as if it were infinite. And as the first step towards truth is to understand our error, Spinoza proceeds to explain the defects of commonsense, or, in other words, of that first and unreflected view of the world, which he, like Plato, calls *opinion*. Opinion is a kind of knowledge derived partly from hearsay, and partly from *experientia vaga*. It consists of vague and general conceptions of things, got either from the report of others or from an experience which has not received any special direction from intelligence.

The mind that has not got beyond the stage of opinion, takes things as they present themselves in its individual experience; and its beliefs grow up by association of whatever happens to have been found together in that experience. And as the combining principle of the elements of opinion is individual and not universal, so its conception of the world is at once fragmentary and accidental. It does not see things in their connection with the unity of the whole, and hence it cannot see them in their true relation to each other. "I assert expressly," says Spinoza, "that the mind has no adequate conception either of itself or of external things, but only a confused knowledge of them, so long as it perceives them only in the common order of nature, *i.e.*, so long as it is *externally* determined to contemplate this or that object by the way in which it happens to present itself in experience, and so long as it is not *internally* determined, by the unity of thought in which it considers a number of things, to understand their agreements, differences, and contradictions."[1]

There are two kinds of errors which are usually supposed to exclude each other, but which Spinoza

[1] *Eth.* i. 29 Schol.

finds to be united in opinion. These are the errors of abstraction and imagination; the former exhibits its vice by defect, the latter its vice by excess. On the one hand, opinion is abstract and one-sided; it is defective in knowledge and takes hold of things only at one point. On the other hand, and just because of this abstractness and one-sidedness, it is forced to give an artificial completeness and independence to that which is essentially fragmentary and dependent. The word abstract is misleading, in so far as we are wont to associate with abstraction the idea of a mental effort by which parts are separated from a given whole; but it may be applied without violence to any imperfect conception, in which things that are really elements of a greater whole are treated as if they were *res completæ*, independent objects, complete in themselves. And in this sense the ordinary consciousness of man is often the victim of abstractions, when it supposes itself most of all to be dealing with realities. For, although the essences and substances of the schoolman may delude him, he cannot think these notions clearly, without seeing that they are only abstract elements of reality, and that they have a meaning only in relation to the other elements of it. But common sense remains unconscious of its abstractness, because imagination gives a kind of substantiality to the fragmentary and limited, and so makes it possible to conceive it as an independent reality. Pure intelligence, seeing the part as it is in itself, could never see it but as a part. Thought, when it rises to clearness and distinctness in regard to any finite object, must at once discern its relation to other finite objects and to the whole, —must discern, in Spinozistic language, that it is "modal" and not "real." But though it is not possible to *think* the part as a whole, it is possible to picture it as a whole. The limited image that fills the mind's eye seems to need nothing else for its reality. We cannot think a house clearly and distinctly in all the connection of its parts with each other, without seeing its necessary relation to the earth on which it stands, to the pressure of the atmosphere, etc. The very circumstances by which the possibility of such an existence is explained, make it impossible to conceive it apart from other things. But nothing hinders my mind from resting on a house by itself as a complete picture. Imagination represents things in the externality of space and time, and is subjected to no other conditions except those of space and time. Hence it can begin anywhere, and stop anywhere. For the same cause it can mingle and confuse together all manner of inconsistent forms—can imagine a man with a horse's head, a candle blazing in vacuo, a speaking tree, a man changed into an animal. There may be elements in the nature of these things that would prevent such combinations; but these elements are not necessarily present to the ordinary consciousness, the abstractness of whose conceptions leaves it absolutely at the mercy of imagination or accidental association. To thought in this stage anything is possible that can be pictured. On the other hand, as knowledge advances, this freedom of combination becomes limited. "The less the mind understands and the more it perceives, the greater is its power of fiction: and the more it understands, the narrower is the limitation of that power. For just as, in the moment of consciousness, we cannot imagine that we do not think, so, when once we have apprehended the nature of body, we cannot conceive of a fly of infinite size, and when once we know the nature of a soul, we cannot think of it as a square, though we may use the words that express these ideas."[1] Thus, according to Spinoza, the range of possibility narrows as knowledge widens, until to perfected knowledge possibility is lost in necessity.

From these considerations, it follows that all thought is imperfect which stops short of the absolute unity of all things. Our first imperfect notion of things, as isolated from each other or connected only by co-existence and succession, is a mere imagination of them. It is a fictitious substantiation of isolated moments which in reality cannot exist apart. Knowledge, so far as it deals with the finite, is engaged in a continual process of self-correction which can never be completed; for at every step there is an element of falsity, in so far as the mind rests in the contemplation of a certain number of the elements of the world, as if they constituted a complete whole by themselves, whereas they are only a part, the conception of which has to be modified at the next step by considering its relation to the other parts. Thus we rise from individuals of the first to individuals of the second order, and we cannot stop short of the idea of "all nature as one individual whose

[1] *De Emend.* viii. § 58.

parts vary through an infinite number of modes, without change of the whole individual."[1] At first we think of pieces of matter as independent individuals, either because we can picture them separately, or because they preserve a certain proportion or relation of parts through their changes. But on further consideration, these apparent substances sink into modes, each of which is dependent on all the others. All nature is bound together by necessary law, and not an atom could be other than it is, without the change of the whole world. Hence it is only in the whole world that there is any true individuality or substance. And the same principle applies to the minds of men. Their individuality is a mere semblance caused by our abstracting from their conditions. Isolate the individual man, and he will not display the character of a thinking being at all. His whole spiritual life is bound up with his relations to other minds, past and present. He has such a life only in and through that universal life, of which he is so infinitesimal a part that his own contribution to it is as good as nothing. " *Vis qua homo in existendo perseverat*

[1] *Eth.* ii. Lemma 7, Schol.

limitata est, et a potentia causarum externarum infinite superatur." [1] What can be called his own? His body is a link in a cyclical chain of movement which involves all the matter of the world, and which as a whole remains without change through all change of the parts. His mind is a link in a great movement of thought, which makes him the momentary organ and expression of one of its phases. His very consciousness of self is marred by a false abstraction, above which he must rise ere he can know himself as he really is.

"Let us imagine," says Spinoza in his fifteenth letter, "a little worm living in blood, which has vision enough to discern the particles of blood, lymph, etc., and reason enough to observe how one particle is repelled by another with which it comes into contact, or communicates a part of its own motion to it. Such a worm would live in the blood as we do in this part of the universe, and would regard each particle of it, not as a part, but as a whole, nor could it know how all the parts are influenced by the universal nature of the blood, and are obliged to accommodate themselves to each other according to a fixed law.

[1] *Eth.* iv. 3.

For if we suppose that there are no causes outside of the blood which could communicate new motions to it, and no space beyond the blood, nor any other bodies to which its particles could transfer their motion, it is certain that the blood as a whole would always maintain its present state, and its particles would suffer no other variations than those which may be inferred from the given relation of the motion of blood to lymph, chyle, etc. And thus the blood would require to be considered always as a whole and not as a part. But since there are many other causes which influence the laws of the nature of blood, and are in turn influenced thereby, other motions and other variations must arise in the blood which are not due to the reciprocal relation of the motion of its parts, but also to the relation between that motion and external causes. And therefore we cannot consider the blood as a whole, but only as a part of a greater whole."

"Now we can think, and indeed ought to think, of all natural bodies in the same manner in which we have thought of this blood, for all bodies are surrounded by other bodies, and reciprocally determine and are determined by them to exist and operate in a fixed and definite way, so as to preserve the same ratio of motion and rest in the whole universe. Hence it follows that every body, in so far as it exists under a certain definite modification, ought to be considered as merely a part of the whole universe, which agrees with its whole, and thereby is in intimate union with all the other parts; and since the nature of the universe is not limited like that of the blood, but absolutely infinite, it is clear that by this nature with its infinite powers, the parts are modified in an infinite number of ways, and compelled to pass through an infinity of variations. Moreover, when I think of the universe as a substance, I conceive of a still closer union of each part with the whole; for, as I have elsewhere shown, it is the nature of substance to be infinite, and therefore every single part belongs to the nature of the corporeal substance, so that apart therefrom it neither can exist nor be conceived. And as to the human mind, I think of it also as a part of nature; for I think of nature as having in it an infinite power of thinking, which, as infinite, contains in itself the idea of all nature, and whose thoughts run parallel with all existence."

From this point of view it is obvious that our knowledge of things cannot be real and adequate, except in so far as it is determined by the idea of the whole, and proceeds from the whole to the parts. A knowledge that proceeds from part to part must always be imperfect; it must remain external to its object, it must deal in abstractions or mere *entia rationis*, which it may easily be led to mistake for realities. Hence Spinoza, like Plato, distinguishes *ratio*, whose movement is regressive (from effect to cause, from variety to unity), from *scientia intuitiva*, whose movement is progressive, which "proceeds from the adequate idea of certain of God's attributes to an adequate knowledge of the nature of things."[1] The latter alone deserves to be called science in the highest sense of the term. For "in order that our mind may correspond to the exemplar of nature, it must develop all its ideas from the idea which represents the origin and source of nature, so that that idea may appear as the source of all other ideas."[2] The regressive mode of knowledge has its highest value in preparing for the progressive. The knowledge of the finite, ere it can become perfectly adequate, must

[1] *Eth.* ii. 40, Schol. 2.   [2] *De Emend.* vii. § 42.

be absorbed and lost in the knowledge of the infinite. In a remarkable passage in the *Ethics*, Spinoza declares that the defect of the common consciousness of men lies not so much in their ignorance, either of the infinite or of the finite, as in their incapacity for bringing the two thoughts together, so as to put the latter in its proper relation to the former. All are ready to confess that God is the cause both of the existence and of the nature of things created, but they do not realize what is involved in this confession. Hence they treat created things as if they were substances, that is, as if they were Gods. "Thus while they are contemplating finite things, they think of nothing less than of the divine nature: and again when they turn to consider the divine nature, they think of nothing less than of their former fictions on which they have built up the knowledge of finite things, as if these things could contribute nothing to our understanding of the divine nature. Hence it is not wonderful that they are always contradicting themselves."[1] As Spinoza says elsewhere, it belongs to the very nature of the human mind to know God; for, if we

[1] *Eth.* ii. 10, Schol. 2.

did not know God, we could not know anything else. The idea of the absolute unity is involved in the idea of every particular thing; but the generality of men, deluded by sense and imagination, are unable to bring this implication into clear consciousness, and hence their knowledge of God does not modify their view of the finite. It is the business of philosophy to correct this defect, to transform our conceptions of the finite by relating it to the infinite, to complement and complete the partial knowledge produced by individual experience by bringing it into connection with the idea of the whole. And the vital question which Spinoza himself prompts us to ask is, how far and in what way this transformation is effected in the Spinozistic philosophy.

There are two great steps in the transformation of knowledge by the idea of unity as that idea is conceived by Spinoza. The first step involves a change of the conception of individual finite things, by which they lose their individuality, their character as independent substances, and come to be regarded as modes of the infinite. But secondly, this negation of the finite as such is not conceived as implying the negation of the distinction between mind and matter. Mind and matter still retain that absolute opposition which they had in the philosophy of Des Cartes, even after all limits have been removed. And therefore in order to reach the absolute unity, and transcend the Cartesian dualism, a second step is necessary, by which the independent substantiality of mind and matter is withdrawn, and they are reduced into attributes of the one infinite substance. Let us examine these steps successively.

The method by which the finite is reduced into a mode of the infinite has already been partially explained. Spinoza follows to its legitimate result the metaphysical or logical principles of Des Cartes and Malebranche. According to the former, as we have seen, the finite presupposes the infinite, and, indeed, so far as it is real, it is identical with the infinite. The infinite is absolute reality, because it is pure affirmation, because it is that which *negationem nullam involvit*. The finite is distinguished from it simply by its limit, *i.e.*, by its wanting something which the infinite has. At this point Spinoza takes up the argument. If the infinite be the real, and

CARTESIANISM. 353

the finite, so far as it is distinguished therefrom, the unreal, then the supposed substantiality or individuality of finite beings is an illusion. In itself the finite is but an abstraction, to which imagination has given an apparent independence. All limitation or determination is negative, and in order to apprehend positive reality, we must abstract from limits. By denying the negative, we reach the affirmative; by annihilating finitude, and so undoing the illusory work of the imagination, we reach the indeterminate or unconditioned being which alone truly is. All division, distinction, and relation are but *entia rationis*. Imagination and abstraction can give to them, as they can give to mere negation and nothingness, "a local habitation and a name," but they have no objective meaning, and in the highest knowledge, in the *scientia intuitiva*, which deals only with reality, they must entirely disappear.

Hence to reach the truth as to matter, we must free ourselves from all such ideas as figure or number, measure or time, which imply the separation and relation of parts. Thus in his 50th letter, in answer to some question about figure, Spinoza says, "to prove that figure is negation, and not anything positive, we need only consider that the whole of matter conceived indefinitely, or in its infinity, can have no figure; but that figure has a place only in finite or determinate bodies. He who says that he perceives figure, says only that he has before his mind a limited thing and the manner in which it is limited. But this limitation does not pertain to a thing in its 'esse,' but contrariwise in its 'non-esse' (*i.e.*, it signifies, not that some positive quality belongs to the thing, but that something is wanting to it). Since, then, figure is but limitation, and limitation is but negation, we cannot say that figure is anything." The same kind of reasoning is elsewhere (*Epist.* 29) applied to solve the difficulties connected with the divisibility of space or extension. Really, according to Spinoza, extension is indivisible, though modally it is divisible. In other words, parts *ad infinitum* may be taken in space by the abstracting mind, but these parts have no separate existence. You cannot rend space, or take one part of it out of its connection with other parts. Hence arises the impossibility of asserting *either* that there is an infinite number of parts in space, *or* that there is not. The solution of the antinomy is that neither alternative is true. There are many things *quæ nullo numero explicari possunt*, and to understand these things we must abstract altogether from the idea of number. The contradiction arises entirely from the application of that idea to the infinite. We cannot say that space has a finite number of parts, for every finite space must be conceived as itself included in infinite space. Yet, on the other hand, an infinite number is an absurdity; it is a number which is not a number. We escape the difficulty only when we see that number is a category inapplicable to the infinite, and this to Spinoza means that it is not applicable to reality, that it is merely an abstraction, or *ens imaginationis*.

The same method which solves the difficulties connected with the nature of matter, is applied to mind. Here also we reach the reality, or thing in itself, by abstracting from all determination. All conceptions, therefore, that involve the independence of the finite, all conceptions of good, evil, freedom, and responsibility disappear. When Blyenbergh accuses Spinoza of making God the author of evil, Spinoza answers that evil is an *ens rationis* that has no existence for God. "Evil is not something positive, but a state of privation, something that exists not in relation to the divine, but simply in relation to the human intelligence. It is a conception that arises from that generalizing tendency of our minds, which leads us to bring all beings that have the external form of man under one and the same definition, and to suppose that they are all equally capable of the highest perfection which we can deduce from such a definition. When, therefore, we find an individual whose works are not consistent with this perfection, straightway we judge that he is deprived of it, or that he is diverging from his own nature,—a judgment we should never make if we had not thus referred him to a general definition, and supposed him to be possessed of the nature it defines. But since God does not know things abstractly, or through such general definitions, and since there cannot be more reality in things than the divine intelligence and power bestows upon them, it manifestly follows that the defect which belongs to finite things, cannot be called a privation in relation to the intelligence of God, but only in relation to the intelligence of man."[1] Thus evil and good vanish when we consider things *sub specie æternitatis*, because they are categories that imply a certain independence in finite beings. For the idea of a moral standard implies a relation of man to the absolute good, a relation of the finite to the infinite, in which the finite is not simply lost and absorbed in the infinite.

But Spinoza can admit no such relation. In the presence of the infinite the finite disappears, for it exists only by abstraction and negation: or it *seems* to us to exist, not because of what is present to our thoughts, but because of what is not present to them. As we think ourselves free, because we are conscious of our actions but not of their causes, so we think that we have an individual existence, because the infinite intelligence is not wholly but only partially realized in us. But as we cannot really divide space, though we can think of a part of it, so neither can we place any real division in the divine intelligence. In this way we can understand how Spinoza is able to speak of the

[1] *Epist.* 32.

human mind as part of the infinite thought of God, and of the human body as part of the infinite extension of God, while yet he asserts that the divine substance is simple, and not made up of parts. So far as they exist, they must be conceived as parts of the divine substance, but when we look directly at that divine substance, their separate existence altogether disappears.

It has, however, been already mentioned that this ascending movement of abstraction does not at once and directly bring Spinoza to the absolute unity of substance. The principle that "determination is negation," and that therefore the absolute reality is to be found only in the indeterminate, would lead us to expect this conclusion; but the Cartesian dualism prevents Spinoza from reaching it. Mind and matter are so absolutely opposed, that even when we take away all limit and determination from both, they still retain their distinctness. Raised to infinity, they still refuse to be identified. We are forced, indeed, to take from them their substantial or substantive existence, for there can be no other substance but God, who includes all reality in Himself. But though reduced to attributes of a common substance, the difference of thought and extension is insoluble. The independence of individual finite things disappears whenever we substitute thought for imagination, but even to pure intelligence, extension remains extension, and thought remains thought.

Spinoza seems therefore reduced to a dilemma; he cannot surrender either the unity or the duality of things, yet he cannot relate them to each other. The only course left open to him is to conceive each attribute in its turn as the whole substance, and to regard their difference as the difference of expression. As the patriarch was called by the two names of Jacob and Israel, under different aspects, each of which included the whole reality of the man, so our minds apprehend the absolute substance in two ways, each of which expresses its whole nature.[1] In this way the extremes of absolute identity and absolute difference seem to be reconciled. There is a complete parallelism of thought and extension, *ordo et connexio idearum idem est ac ordo et connexio rerum*,[2] yet there is also a complete independence and absence of relation

[1] *Epist.* 27.   [2] *Eth.* ii. 7.

between them, for each is the whole. A thing in one expression cannot be related to itself in another expression. Hence in so far as we look at the substance under the attribute of thought, we must take no account of extension, and in so far as we look at it under the attribute of extension, we must equally refuse to take any account of thought. This parallelism may be best illustrated by Spinoza's account of the relation of the human soul and body. The soul is the idea of the body, and the body is the object of the soul, whatever is in the one really is in the other ideally; yet this relation of object and subject does not imply any connection. The motions and changes of the body have to be accounted for partly by itself, partly by the influence of other bodies; and the thoughts of the soul in like manner have to be accounted for partly by what God thinks as constituting the individual mind, and partly by what He thinks as constituting the minds of other individuals. But to account for thought by the motions of the body, or for the motions of the body by thought, is to attempt to bridge the impassable gulf between thought and extension. It involves the double absurdity of accounting for a thing by itself, and of accounting for it by that which has nothing in common with it.

In one point of view, this theory of Spinoza deserves the highest praise for that very characteristic which probably excited most odium against it at the time it was first published, namely, its exaltation of matter. It is the mark of an imperfect spiritualism to hide its eyes from outward nature, and to shrink from the material as impure and defiling. But its horror and fear are proofs of weakness; it flies from an enemy it cannot overcome. Spinoza's bold identification of spirit and matter, God and nature, contains in it the germ of a higher idealism than can be found in any philosophy that asserts the claims of the former at the expense of the latter. A system that begins by making nature godless, will inevitably end, as Schelling once said, in making God unnatural. The expedients by which Des Cartes keeps matter at a distance from God, were intended to maintain His pure spirituality; but their ultimate effect was seen in his reduction of the spiritual nature to mere will. As Christianity has its superiority over other religions in this, that it does not end with the opposition of the human to the divine, the natural to the spiritual, but ultimately reconciles them, so a true idealism must vindicate its claims by absorbing materialism into itself. It was therefore a true instinct of philosophy that led Spinoza to raise matter to the co-equal of spirit, and at the same time to protest against the Cartesian conception of matter as mere inert mass, moved only by impulse from without. "What were a God that only impelled the world from without?" says Goethe. "It becomes Him to stir it by an inward energy, to involve nature in Himself, Himself in nature, so that that which lives and moves and has a being in Him can never feel the want of His power or His spirit."

While, however, Spinoza thus escapes some of the inconsequences of Des Cartes, the contradiction that was *implicit* in the Cartesian system between the duality and the unity, the attributes and the substance, in his system becomes *explicit*. When so much emphasis is laid upon the unity of substance, it becomes more difficult to explain the difference of the attributes. The result is, that Spinoza is forced to account for it, not by the nature of substance itself, but by the nature of the intelligence to which it is revealed. "By substance," he says, "I understand that which is in itself, and is conceived through itself. By attribute I understand the same thing, *nisi quod attributum dicatur respectu intellectus substantiæ certum talem naturam tribuentis.*"[1] Hence we are naturally led with Erdmann to think of the intelligence dividing the substance as a kind of prism that breaks the white light into different colours, through each of which the same world is seen, only with a different aspect. But if the intelligence in itself is but a mode of one of the attributes, how can it be itself the source of their distinction?

The key to this difficulty is that Spinoza has really, and almost in spite of his logical principles, two opposite conceptions of substance, between which he alternates without ever bringing them to a unity. On the one hand, in accordance with the principle that determination is negation, substance must be taken as that which is utterly indeterminate, an Absolute Being, which we can characterise only by denying of it

[1] *Epist.* 27.

everything that we assert of the finite. In this
view, no predicate can be applied univocally to
God and to the creatures; He differs from them,
not only in existence, but in essence.[1] If we
follow out this view to its legitimate result, God
is withdrawn into His own absolute unity, and no
difference of attributes can be ascribed to Him,
except in respect of something else than Himself.
It is owing to the defects of our intelligence that
He appears under different forms or expressions;
in Himself He is pure Being, without form or expression at all. But, on the other hand, it is to
be observed, that while Spinoza really proceeds
by abstraction and negation, he does not *mean* to
do so. The abstract is to him the unreal and
imaginary, and what he means by substance is not
simply Being in general,—the conception that remains when we omit all that distinguishes the
particulars,—but the absolute totality of things,
conceived as a unity in which all particular existence is included and subordinated. Hence at a
single stroke the indeterminate passes into the
most determinate Being, the Being with no attributes at all passes into the Being constituted by

[1] *Eth.* i. 17, Schol.

an infinite number of attributes. And while, under the former conception, the defect of our intelligence seemed to be that it divided the substance, or saw a difference of attributes in its absolute unity, under the second conception its defect lies in its apprehending only *two* out of the infinite multitude of these attributes.

To do justice to Spinoza, therefore, we must distinguish between the actual effect of his logic and its effect as he conceived it. The actual effect of his logic is to dissolve all things in the ultimate abstraction of Being, from which we can find no way back to the concrete. But his intent was simply to relate all the parts to that absolute unity which is the presupposition of all thought and being, and so to arrive at the most concrete and complete idea of the reality of things. He failed to see what is involved in his own principle that "determination is negation"; for if affirmation is impossible without negation, then the attempt to divorce the two from each other, the attempt to find a purely affirmative being, must necessarily end in confusing the barest of all abstractions with the unity of all things. But even when the infinite substance is defined as the negative of the finite, the idea of the finite becomes an essential element in the conception of the infinite. Even the Pantheist, who says that God is what finite things are not, recognises in spite of himself that God has a relation to finite things. Finite things may in his eyes have no positive relation to God, yet they have a negative relation; it is through their evanescence and transitoriness, through their nothingness, that the eternal, the infinite reality alone is revealed to him.

Spinoza is quite conscious of this process, conscious that he reaches the affirmation of substance by a negation of what he conceives as the purely negative and unreal existence of finite things: but as he regards the assertion of the finite as merely an illusion due to *our* imagination, so he regards the correction of this illusion, the negation of the finite as a movement of reflection which belongs merely to *our* intelligence, and has nothing to do with the nature of substance in itself. We find the true affirmation by the negation of the negative, but in itself affirmation has no relation to negation. Hence his absolute being is the dead all-absorbing substance and not the self-revealing spirit. It is the being without determination, and not the being that determines itself. There is no reason in the nature of substance why it should have either attributes or modes; neither individual finite things nor the general distinction of mind and matter can be deduced from it. The descending movement of thought is not what Spinoza himself said it should be, an evolution, but simply an external and empirical process by which the elements dropped in the ascending movement of abstraction are taken up again with a merely nominal modification. For the sole change in the conception of mind and matter in general and in the conception of individual minds and bodies, which results from their reference to the idea of God, is that they lose their substantive character and become adjectives. Aristotle objected to Plato that his ideas were merely αἰσθητὰ ἀΐδια, that is, that his idealisation of the world was merely superficial, and left the things idealised very much what they were before to the sensuous consciousness; and the same may be said of Spinoza's negation of finite things. It was an external and imperfect negation, which did not transform the idea of the finite, but merely substituted the names of attributes and modes for the names of general and individual substances.

The same defective logic, by which the movement of thought in determining the substance is regarded as altogether external to the substance itself, is seen again in Spinoza's conceptions of the relations of the attributes to each other. Adopting the Cartesian opposition of mind and matter, he does not see, any more than Des Cartes, that in their opposition they are correlative. Or if he did see it (as seems possible from a passage in his earliest treatise),[1] he regarded the correlation as merely subjective, merely belonging to our thought. They are to him only the two attributes which we happen to know, out of the infinite number belonging to God. There is no necessity that the substance should manifest itself in just these attributes and no others; for abstract substance is equally receptive of all determinations, and equally indifferent to them all. Just because the unity is merely generic, the differences are accidental, and do not form by their union any complete whole. If Spinoza had seen that matter in itself is the correlative opposite of mind in itself, he need not have sought by abstracting from the difference of these elements to reach a unity which is manifested in that very

[1] *Tractatus de Deo et homine,* ii. 19.

difference, and his absolute would have been not substance but spirit.

This idea he never reached, but we find him approximating to it in two ways. On the one hand, he condemns the Cartesian conception of matter as passive and self-external, or infinitely divisible—as, in short, the mere opposite of thought.[1] And sometimes he insists on the parallelism of extension and thought at the expense of their opposition in a way that almost anticipates the assertion by Leibniz of the essential identity of mind and matter. On the other hand, he recognises that this parallelism is not complete. Thought is not like a picture; it is conscious, and conscious not only of itself, but of extension. It transcends therefore the absolute distinction between itself and the other attributes. It is only because he cannot rid himself of the phantom of an extended matter, as a thing in itself which is entirely different from the idea of it, that Spinoza is prevented from recognising in mind that unity which transcends all distinctions, even its own distinction from matter. As it is, his main reason for saying that intelligence is not an attribute of God, but merely a

[1] *Epist.* 70.

mode, seems to be this, that the thought of God must be conceived as producing its own object, *i.e.*, as transcending the distinction of subject and object which is necessary to our intelligence.[1] But this argument of itself points to a concrete quite as much as to an abstract unity. It is as consistent with the idea of absolute spirit as with that of absolute substance. Spinoza's deliberate and formal doctrine is undoubtedly the latter; but he constantly employs expressions which imply the former, as when he speaks of God as *causa sui*. The higher idea inspires him, though his consciousness only embraces the lower idea.

The ethical philosophy of Spinoza is determined by the same principles and embarrassed by the same difficulties as his metaphysics. In it also we find the same imperfect conception of the relation of the positive to the negative elements, and, as a consequence, the same confusion of the highest unity of thought, the affirmation that subordinates and transcends all negation with mere abstract affirmation. Or, to put the same thing in ethical language, Spinoza teaches a morality which is in every point the opposite of asceticism,

[1] *Eth.* i. 17, Schol.

a morality of self-assertion or self-seeking, and not of self-denial. The *conatus sese conservandi* is to him the supreme principle of virtue;[1] yet this self-seeking is supposed, under the guidance of reason, to identify itself with the love of man and the love of God, and to find blessedness not in the reward of virtue, but in virtue itself. It is only confusion of thought and false mysticism that could object to this result on the ground of the element of self still preserved in the *amor Dei intellectualis*. For it is just the power of identifying himself with that which is wider and higher than his individual being that makes morality possible to man. But the difficulty lies in this, that Spinoza will not admit the negative element, the element of mortification or sacrifice, into morality at all, even as a moment of transition. For him there is no dead self, by which we may rise to higher things, no losing of life that we may find it. The negative is nothing; it is evil in the only sense in which evil exists, and cannot be the source of good. The higher affirmation of our own being, the higher seeking of ourselves which is identical with the love of God, must

[1] *Eth.* iv. 22, Schol.

therefore be regarded as nothing distinct in kind from that first seeking of our natural self which in Spinoza's view belongs to us in common with the animals, and indeed in common with all beings whatever. It must be regarded merely as a direct development and extension of the same thing. The main interest of the Spinozistic ethics therefore lies in observing by what steps he accomplishes this transition, while excluding altogether the idea of a real division of the higher and the lower life, the spirit and flesh, and of a conflict in which the former is developed through the sacrifice of the latter.

Finite creatures exist as modes of the divine substance, only so far as they partake in the infinite, or, what is the same thing with Spinoza, in the purely affirmative or self-affirming nature of God. They therefore must also be self-affirming. They can never limit themselves; their limit lies in this, that they are not identified with the infinite substance which expresses itself also in other modes. In other words, the limit of any finite creature, that which makes it finite, lies without it, and its own existence, so far as it goes, must be pure self-assertion and self-seeking. *Unaquæque res quantum in se est in suo esse perseverare conatur*, and this *conatus* is its very essence or inmost nature.[1] In the animals this *conatus* takes the form of appetite, in man of desire, which is "appetite with the consciousness of it."[2] But this constitutes no essential difference between appetite and desire, for "whether a man be conscious of his appetite or no, the appetite remains one and the same thing."[3] Man therefore, like the animals, is purely self-asserting and self-seeking. He can neither know nor will anything but his own being, or if he knows or wills anything else, it must be something involved in his own being. If he knows other beings, or seeks their good, it must be because their existence and their good are involved in his own. If he loves and knows God, it must be because he cannot know himself without knowing God, or find his supreme good anywhere but in God.

What at first makes the language difficult to us is the identification of will and intelligence. Both are represented as affirming their objects. Des Cartes had prepared the way for this when

[1] *Eth.* iii. 6, 7.   [2] *Eth.* iii. 9.
[3] *Eth.* iii. Affect. Def. 1.

he treated the will as the faculty of judging or giving assent to certain combinations of ideas, and distinguished it from the purely intellectual faculties by which the ideas are apprehended. By this distinction he had, as he supposed, secured a place for human freedom. Admitting that intelligence is under a law of necessity, he claimed for the will a certain latitude or liberty of indifference, a power of giving or withholding assent in all cases where the relations of ideas were not absolutely clear and distinct. Spinoza points out that there is no ground for such a distinction, that the acts of apprehension and judgment cannot be separated from each other. "In the mind there is no volition, *i.e.*, no affirmation or negation which is not immediately involved in the idea it apprehends," and therefore "intellect and will are one and the same thing."[1] If, then, there is no freedom except the liberty of indifference, freedom is impossible. Man, like all other beings and things, is under an absolute law of necessity. All the actions of his will, as well as of his intelligence, are but different forms of the self-assertive tendency to which he cannot but yield, because it is one with

[1] *Eth.* ii. 49.

his very being, or only ideally distinguishable therefrom.

There is, however, another idea of liberty. Liberty as the opposite of necessity is an absurdity —it is impossible for either God or man; but liberty as the opposite of slavery is possible, and it is actually possessed by God. The divine liberty consists in this, that God acts from the necessity of His own nature alone, and is not in any way determined from without. And the great question of ethics is, How far can man partake in this liberty? At first it would seem impossible that he should partake in it. He is a finite being, whose power is infinitely surpassed by the power of other beings to which he is related. His body acts only as it is acted on, and his mind cannot therefore apprehend his body, except as affected by other things. His self-assertion and self-seeking are therefore confused with the asserting and seeking of other things, and are never pure. His thought and activity cannot be understood except through the influence of other things which lie outside of his consciousness, and upon which his will has no influence. He cannot know clearly and distinctly either himself or anything else; how then can he know his own good or determine himself by the idea of it?

The answer is the answer of Des Cartes, that the apprehension of any finite thing involves the adequate idea of the infinite and eternal nature of God.[1] This is the primary object of intelligence, in which alone is grounded the possibility of knowing either ourselves or anything else. In so far as our knowledge is determined by this idea, or by the ideas of other things, which are referred to this idea and seen in its light, in so far its action flows from an internal and not an external necessity. In so far, on the other hand, as we are determined by the affections of the body, *i.e.*, by ideas in which the nature of our own body and the nature of other things are confused together, in so far we are determined by an external necessity. Or, to put the same thing in what has been shown to be merely another way of expression, in so far as we are determined by pure intelligence we are free, but in so far as we are determined by opinion and imagination we are slaves.

From these premises it is easy to see what form the opposition of reason and passion must necessarily take with Spinoza. The passions belong to

[1] *Eth.* ii. 45.

our nature as finite; they are grounded on, or rather are but another form of inadequate ideas; but we are free only in so far as our ideas either immediately are, or can be made, adequate. Our idea of God is adequate *ex vi termini;* our ideas of the affections of our body are inadequate, but can be made adequate in so far as they are referred to the idea of God. And as the idea of God is purely affirmative, this reference to the idea of God implies the elimination of the negative element from the ideas of the affections of the body, "for nothing that is positive in a false idea is removed by the presence of truth as such."[1] Brought into contact with the idea of God, all ideas become true and adequate, by the removal of the negative or false element in them. The idea of God is, as it were, the touchstone which distinguishes the gold from the dross. It enables us to detect the higher spiritual element in the natural passions, and to sever the element belonging to that pure love of self, which is identical with the love of perfection, from the elements belonging to that impure love of our own finite individuality as such, which is identical with the love of evil.

[1] *Eth.* iv. 1.

The imperfection in Spinoza's development of this principle has already been indicated. It is in fact the same imperfection which runs through his whole system. Just as he supposed that the ideas of finite things were at once made consistent with the idea of the infinite when he had named them modes, so here his conception of the change through which selfish natural desire must pass in order to become spiritual, is far too superficial and external. Hence he has no sympathy with asceticism, but treats it, like Bentham, as a *torva et tristis superstitio*. Joy is the "transition from less to greater perfection," and cannot be but good; pain is the "transition from greater to less perfection," and cannot be but evil. The revolt against the mediæval opposition of nature and spirit is visible in many of his sayings. "No Deity who is not envious can delight in my weakness or hurts, or can regard as virtues those fears and sighs and tears which are the signs of the mind's weakness; but contrariwise, the greater is our joy, the greater is our progress to perfection, and our participation in the divine nature."[1] "A free man thinks of nothing so little as of death, his wisdom

[1] *Eth.* iv. 45, Schol.

is a meditation not of death but of life."[1] The same idea, combining with the idea of necessity, leads him to condemn repentance and pity, as well as pride and humility. Unconsciously, Spinoza reproduces the principle of asceticism, while in words he utterly rejects it. For though he tells us that pure self-complacency is the highest thing we can hope, yet from this self-complacency all regard to the finite individuality of the subject is eliminated. *Qui Deum amat, conari non potest ut Deus ipsum contra amet.* In like manner, he absolutely condemns all hatred, envy, rivalry, and ambition, as springing out of an over-estimate of those finite things which only one can possess, while the highest good is that which is enjoyed the more easily and fully the greater the number of participants. Yet Spinoza's exaltation of the social life, and of the love that binds it together, is too like the Buddhist's universal charity that embraces all creatures, and all creatures equally. Both are based on an abstraction from all that is individual, only the Buddhist's abstraction goes a step further, and erases even the distinction between man and the animals. Spinoza felt the

[1] *Eth.* iv. 67.

pressure of this all-levelling logic when he said, "I confess I cannot understand how spirits express God more than the other creatures, for I know that between the finite and the infinite there is no proportion, and that the distinction between God and the most excellent of created things differs not a whit from the distinction between him and the lowest and meanest of them."[1] As Pope said, God is "as full, as perfect in a hair as heart"; in all finite things there is a ray of divinity, and in nothing more than a ray. Yet in another epistle, Spinoza contradicts this view, and declares that, while he does not consider it necessary to "know Christ after the flesh, he does think it is necessary to know the eternal Son of God, *i.e.*, God's eternal wisdom, which is manifested in all things, but chiefly in the mind of man, and most of all in Christ Jesus."[2] In the *Ethics* Spinoza treats the distinction of man and the animals as an absolute distinction, and, forgetful of the parallelism of the attributes, he asserts that the human soul cannot all be destroyed along with the body, for that there is something of it which is eternal. Yet from this eternity we must of course

[1] *Epist.* 57. [2] *Epist.* 21.

eliminate all notion of the consciousness of the finite self as such.

At this point, therefore, the two opposite streams of Spinoza's thought, the positive method he *intends* to pursue, and the negative or abstracting method he really *does* pursue, meet in irreconcilable contradiction. The finite must be related to the infinite so as to preserve all that is in it of reality; and therefore we must abstract from its limit, *i.e.*, from the negative element in it. But it turns out that with this abstraction the positive also disappears, and God becomes all in all in a sense that absolutely excludes the existence of the finite. "The mind's intellectual love of God," says Spinoza, "is the very love wherewith God loves Himself, not in so far as He is infinite, but in so far as He can be expressed by the essence of the human mind, considered under the form of eternity; *i.e.*, the mind's intellectual love of God is part of the infinite love wherewith God loves Himself."[1] This double "in so far," which returns so frequently in Spinoza, just conceals for a moment the contradiction of two streams of thought, one of which must be swallowed up by the other, if they are once allowed to meet.

[1] *Eth.* v. 36.

We have now reviewed the main points of the system, which was the ultimate result of the principles of Des Cartes. The importance of this first movement of modern philosophy lies in its assertion and exhibition of the unity of the intelligible world with itself and with the mind of man. In this point of view, it was the philosophical counterpart of Protestantism; but, like Protestantism in its earliest phase, it passed rapidly from the doctrine that, without the mediation of priest or authority, God can reveal Himself to the spirit of man, to the doctrine that man's spirit is as nothing before God. The divine object seemed too powerful for the subject, who effaced himself before God that he might be strong towards men. But in this natural movement of feeling and thought it was forgotten that a God that effaces the world and the finite spirit by His presence cannot be a living God. Spinoza gives the ultimate expression to this tendency, and at the same time marks its limit, when he says that whatever reality is in the finite is of the infinite. But he is unsuccessful in showing that, on the principles on which he starts, there can be any reality in the finite at all. Yet even if the finite be an illusion, still more if it be better than an illusion, it requires to be accounted for. Spinoza accounts for it neither as illusory nor as real. It was reserved for the following generation of philosophers to assert, in different ways, the reality of the finite, the value of experience, and the futility of abstractions. Spinoza had declared that true knowledge consists in seeing things under the form of eternity; but it is impossible that things can be seen under the form of eternity, unless they have been first seen under the form of time. The one-sided assertion of individuality and difference in the schools of Locke and Leibniz, was the natural complement of the one-sided assertion of universality and unity in the Cartesian school. But when the individualistic tendency of the eighteenth century had exhausted itself, and produced its own refutation in the works of Kant, it was inevitable that the minds of men should again turn to the great philosopher, who, with almost perfect insight working through imperfect logic, first formulated the idea of a unity pre-supposed in and transcending the difference of matter and mind, subject and object.

METAPHYSIC.

THE term metaphysic, originally intended to mark the place of a particular treatise in the collection of Aristotle's works, has, mainly owing to a misunderstanding, survived several other titles, such as "First Philosophy," "Ontology," and "Theology," which Aristotle himself used or suggested. Neo-Platonic mystics interpreted it as signifying that which is not merely "after" but "beyond" physics, and found in it a fit designation for a science which, as they held, could not be attained except by one who had turned his back upon the natural world. And writers of a different tendency in a later time gladly accepted it as a convenient nickname for theories which they regarded as having no basis in experience, in the same spirit in which the great German minister Stein used the analogous title of "metapolitics" for airy and unpractical schemes of social reform. A brief indication of the contents of Aristotle's treatise may enable us to give a general definition of the science which was first distinctly constituted by it, and to determine in what sense the subjects which that science has to consider are beyond nature and experience.

For Aristotle, metaphysic is the science which has to do with Being as such, Being in general, as distinguished from the special sciences which deal with special forms of Being. There are certain questions which, in Aristotle's view, we have a right to ask in regard to everything that presents itself as real. We may ask what is its ideal nature or definition, and what are the conditions of its realisation; we may ask by what or whom it was produced, and for what end; we may ask, in other words, for the formal and the material, for the efficient and the final causes of everything that is. These different questions point to different elements in our notion of Being, elements which may be considered in their general relations apart from any particular case of their union. These, therefore, the first philosophy must investigate.

But, further, this science of being cannot be entirely separated from the science of knowing, but must determine at least its most general principles. For the science that deals with what is most universal in being is, for that very reason, dealing with the objects which are most nearly akin to the intelligence. These, indeed, are not the objects which are first presented to our minds; we begin with the particular, not the universal, with a πρῶτον ἡμῖν which is not πρῶτον φύσει; but science reaches its true form only when the order of thought is made one with the order of nature, and the particular is known through the universal. Yet this conversion or revolution of the intellectual point of view is not to be regarded as an absolute change from error to truth; for Aristotle holds that *nihil est in intellectu quod non prius in sensu*, in the meaning that in sense perception there is already the working of that discriminative intelligence [1] which, beginning in sense perception, with the distinction of particular from particular, can rest only when it has apprehended things in their universal forms or definitions. Looking at know-

[1] Δύναμις κριτική, *Anal. Post.* ii. 99b.

ledge *formally*, the highest law of thought, the law of contradiction (or, as we might call it, to indicate Aristotle's meaning more exactly, the law of definition or distinction), is already implied in the first act of perception by which one thing is distinguished from another. Looking at it *materially*, the reason of man is to be conceived as potentially all that is knowable; *i.e.*, objects are so related to it that for it to know them in their essential definitions is only to know itself. The aim of science, in this view, is to break through the husk of matter, and to apprehend things in their forms, in which they are one with the mind that knows them. Hence also it follows that in rising to the most universal science, the science of being in general, the mind is not leaving the region of immediate experience, in which it is at home, for a far-off region of abstractions. Rather it is returning to itself, apprehending that which is most closely related to itself, and which therefore, though it is late in being made the direct object of investigation, is yet presupposed in all that is, and is known.[1]

[1] What is said here as to the intelligence is partly taken from the *De Anima*. The necessary qualifications of the

Metaphysic, then, is the science which deals with the principles whch are presupposed in all being and knowing, though they are brought to light only by philosophy. One more trait completes the Aristotelian account of it. It is theology, or the science of God. Now God is νόησις νοήσεως, pure self-consciousness, the absolute thought which is one with its object, and He is therefore the first cause of all existence. For, while the world of nature is a world of motion and change, in which form is realised in matter, this process of the finite can be explained only by referring it back to an unmoved mover, in whom there is no distinction of matter and form, and who is, therefore, in Aristotle's view, to be conceived as pure form, the purely ideal or theoretic activity of a consciousness whose object is itself. Such a conception, however, while it secures the independence and absoluteness of the unmoved mover, by detaching from him all relation to what is other than himself, seems to make his connection with the world inexplicable. We can on this theory refer the world to God, but

above general statement of Aristotle's views will be given subsequently.

not God to the world. Hence Aristotle seems sometimes to say that God is the first mover only as He is the last end after which all creation strives, and this leads him to attribute to nature a desire or will which is directed towards the good as its object or end.

Aristotle then brings together in his metaphysic three elements which are often separated from each other, and the connection of which is far from being at once obvious. It is to him the science of the first principles of being. It is also the science of the first principles of knowing. Lastly, it is the science of God, as the beginning and end of all things, the absolute unity of being and thought, in which all the differences of finite thought and existence are either excluded or overcome.

To some this description of the contents of Aristotle's treatise, and especially the last part of it, may seem to be a confirmation of all the worst charges brought against metaphysic. For at both extremes this supposed science seems to deal with that which is beyond experience, and which therefore cannot be verified by it. It takes us back to a beginning, which is prior to the existence as well as to the consciousness of finite objects in time and space, and on to an end, to which no scientific prophecy based upon our consciousness of such objects can reach. In the former aspect of it, it has to do with notions so abstract and general that it seems as if they could not be fixed or tested by reference to any experience, but must necessarily be the playthings of dialectical sophistry. In the latter aspect of it, it entangles us in questions as to the final cause and ultimate meaning of things, questions involving so comprehensive a view of the infinite universe in which we are insignificant parts that it seems as if any attempt to answer them must be for us vain and presumptuous. On both sides, therefore, metaphysic appears to be an attempt to occupy regions which are beyond the habitable space of the intelligible world—to deal with ideas which are either so vague and abstract that they cannot be fastened to any definite meaning, or so complex and far-reaching that they can never by any possibility be verified. For beings like men, fixed within these narrow limits of space and time, the true course, it would seem, is to "cultivate their gardens," asking neither whence they come nor whither they go, or asking it only within the possible limits of history and scientific prophecy. To go back to the beginning or forward to the end, even in a temporal, still more in a metaphysical sense, is beyond our power. That which is πρῶτον φύσει escapes us even more absolutely than the prehistorical and pregeological records of man and his world. That which is ὕστατον φύσει escapes us even more absolutely than the far-off future type of civilisation, which social science vainly endeavours to anticipate. Our state is best pictured by that early Anglican philosopher who compared it to a bird flying through a lighted room " between the night and the night." The true aim of philosophy is, therefore, it would seem, to direct our thoughts to the careful examination and utilisation of the narrow space allotted to us by an inscrutable power, and with scientific self-restraint to refrain from all speculation either on first or on final causes.

The main questions as to the possibility and the nature of metaphysic, according to Aristotle's conception of it, may be summed up under two heads. We may ask whether we can in any sense reach that which is beyond experience, and, if so, whether this "beyond" is a first or a last principle, a precondition or a final cause of nature and experience, or both. The former question branches out into two subordinate questions, according as we look at metaphysic from the objective or the subjective side, or, to express the matter more accurately, according as we consider it in relation to those natural objects which are *merely* objects of knowledge, or in relation to those spiritual objects which are also subjects of knowledge. We shall, therefore, consider metaphysic, *first*, in relation to science in general, and, *secondly*, in relation to the special science of psychology. The latter question has also two aspects; for, while the idea of a first cause or principle points to the connection between metaphysic and logic, the idea of a last principle or final cause connects metaphysic with theology. We shall therefore consider in the *third* place the relation of metaphysic to logic, and in the *fourth* place its relation to religion and the philosophy of religion.

1. *Relation of Metaphysic to Science.* — The beginnings of science and metaphysic are identical, though there is a sense in which it may be admitted that the metaphysical comes before the

scientific or positive era. The first efforts of philosophy grasp at once at the prize of absolute knowledge. No sooner did the Greeks become dissatisfied with the pictorial synthesis of mythology, by which their thoughts were first lifted above the confusion of particular things, than they asked for one universal principle which should explain all things. The Ionic school sought to find some one phenomenon of nature which might be used as the key to all other phenomena. The Eleatics, seeing the futility of making one finite thing the explanation of all other finite things, tried to find that explanation in the very notion of Unity or Being itself. We need not underestimate the speculative value of such bold attempts to sum up all the variety of the world in one idea, but it is obvious that they rather give a name to the problem than solve it, or in other words, that they put the very consciousness of the problem in place of the solution of it. Science is possible only if we can rise from the particular to the universal, from a subjective view of things, as they immediately present themselves to us in perception, to an objective determination of them through laws and principles which have no special relation to any particular set of events or to any one individual subject. But this is only one aspect of the matter. To advance from a conception of the world *in ordine ad individuum* to one *in ordine ad universum*, and so to discount and eliminate what is merely subjective and accidental in our first consciousness of the world, is the beginning of knowledge. But little is gained unless the universal, which we reach through the negation of the particulars, is more than their mere negation; unless it is a law or principle by means of which we can explain the particulars. Now the defect of early philosophy was that its universal was "the one beyond the many," not the "one in the many,"—in other words, that it was not a law or principle by which the particulars subsumed under it could be explained, but simply the abstraction of an element common to them. But the process of knowledge is a process that involves both analysis and synthesis, both negation and reaffirmation of the particulars with which we start. If we exaggerate the former aspect of it, we enter upon the *via negativa* of the mystics, the way of pure abstraction and negation, which would open the mind to the ideal reality of things simply by shutting it to all the perceptions of sensible phenomena. And, if we follow out this method to its legitimate result, we must treat the highest abstraction, the abstraction of Being, as if it were the sum of all reality; and the Neo-Platonic ecstasy in which all distinction, even the distinction of subject and object, is lost as the only attitude of mind in which truth can be apprehended.

In the philosophy of the Socratic school we find the first attempt at a *systematic* as opposed to an *abstract* theory—the first attempt to bring together the one and the many, and so to determine the former that it should throw light upon the latter. Yet even in Plato the tendency to oppose the universal to the particular is stronger than the tendency to relate them to each other, and in some of his dialogues, as, *e.g.*, in the *Phædo*, we find a near approach to that identification of the process of knowledge with abstraction which is the characteristic of mysticism. Aristotle, therefore, had some ground for taking the Platonic principle that "the real is the universal" in a sense which excludes the reality of the individual. Yet, though he detected Plato's error in opposing the universal to the particular, and though, at the same time, he did not entirely lose sight of the truth which Plato had exaggerated, that the particular is intelligible only *through* the universal, Aristotle was not able to escape the influence of that dualism which had marred the philosophy of his predecessor.[1] Hence the effect of his protest against a philosophy of abstraction was partly neutralised by his separation between the divine Being as pure form, and nature as the unity of form and matter, and again by his separation of the pure reason which apprehends the forms of things from the perceptions of sense which deal with forms realised in matter. And after Aristotle's time the tendency of philosophy was more and more to withdraw from contact with experience. The Neo-Platonic philosophy, and the Christian theology which was so strongly influenced by it, contained, indeed, an idea of the reconciliation of God and nature, and hence of form and matter, which must ultimately be fatal to dualism, and therefore to the method of mere abstraction. But the explicit meaning of the philosophy of the Middle Ages was still dualistic, and the mode in which the

---

[1] Cf. Green's Essay on Aristotle, *Works*, Vol. iii.

Aristotelian formulæ were wrought into the substance of Christian doctrine by the Scholastics, tended more and more to conceal that idea of the unity of opposites which was involved in Christianity. Hence mediæval Realism presented, in its most one-sided form, the doctrine that "the real is the universal," meaning by the universal nothing more than the abstract. And, as a natural consequence, the modern insurrection of the scientific spirit against scholasticism took its start from an equally bald and one-sided assertion of the opposite principle, that "the real is the individual," meaning by that the individual of immediate perception. If Platonism had dwelt too exclusively on one aspect of the process of knowledge, viz., that it seeks to rise above the particular, the sensible, the subjective, to the universal, the intelligible, the objective, as if in the latter alone were reality to be found, modern men of science learnt from their first nominalistic teachers to regard the universal as nothing more than an abbreviated expression for the particulars, and science itself as a mere generalisation of the facts of sensible perception. But this view of scientific knowledge, as a mere reaffirmation of what is immediately given in sense, is as imperfect as the opposite theory, which reduces it to the mere negation of what is so given. An ideal world utterly and entirely divorced from the phenomenal, and an ideal world which is simply a repetition of the phenomenal, are equally meaningless. The processes of science have both a negative and a positive side; they involve a negation of the particular as it is immediately presented in sense, but only with a view to its being reaffirmed with a new determination through the universal. The fact, as it is first presented to us, is not the fact as it is; for, though it is from the fact as given that we rise to the knowledge of the law, it is the law that first enables us to understand what the fact really means. Our first consciousness of things is thus, not an immovable foundation upon which science may build, but rather a hypothetical and self-contradictory starting-point of investigation, which becomes changed and transformed as we advance.

The Nominalism of scientific men in modern times is due to two special causes, one of which has already been mentioned. It is partly due to the traditions of a time when mediæval Realism was the great enemy of science. The Baconian protest against the "anticipation of nature" was a relative truth, when it was urged against a class of writers who supposed that true theories could be attained without regard to facts; the Baconian assertion of the necessity of attending to *axiomata media* was the necessary correction of the tendencies of mystics, who supposed that philosophy could attain its end by grasping at once at absolute unity, and contented themselves therefore with a unity which did nothing to explain the differences. But, when the former was turned into the dogmatic assertion that the mind is, or ought to be, passive in the process of knowledge, as having in itself no principle for the explanation of things, and when the latter was turned into the dogmatic assertion that science can only proceed from part to part and never from the whole to the parts, these relative truths became a source of error. And this error was confirmed and increased by the mistaken views of those who first tried to correct it. For these, admitting that scientific truth is entirely derived from external experience, only ventured to assert the existence of *a priori* knowledge alongside of, and in addition to, that which is *a posteriori*. In other words, they sought in inner experience a basis for those beliefs which outward experience seemed unable to support. But this basis was soon found to be treacherous. Introspection, observation of the inner life, as opposed to and distinguished from the outer life, could be only an observation of the facts of the individual consciousness as such; and to base religion and morality on such a foundation was to treat God and right as subjective phenomena, which do not necessarily correspond to any objective reality. Nor was this conclusion really evaded by the assertion of the self-evidencing necessity of such ideas and beliefs, or of the principles upon which they are founded. For this necessity, as a subjective phenomenon, might be accounted for otherwise than by the supposition of their objective validity. Such scepticism, was favoured by the progress of science, which, as it advanced from physics to biology and sociology, became more and more inconsistent with the idea of an absolute breach between inner and outer experience, and narrowed the sphere which had hitherto been reserved for the former. Man, it was urged, is but a part in a greater whole, not exempted from the law of action and reaction which connects all parts of that whole with each other. His individual life contains only a few links in a chain of causation that goes back to a beginning and onward to an end of which he knows nothing. And, as Spinoza says, *vis qua homo in existendo perseverat, limitata est et a causis externis infinite superatur.*[1] Hence to treat ideas which are only states of the individual consciousness as the explanation of the world, instead of treating them as phenomena to be explained by its relation to that world, seemed to be an absurdity. The particular beliefs and tendencies of the mind were to be regarded, not as ultimate facts in reference to which everything is to be interpreted, but rather as facts which must themselves be referred to more general causes and laws. It thus appeared that the attempt to divide truth into an *a posteriori* and an *a priori* part, the latter of which should find its evidence in an inner experience as the former in an outer experience, is an illusive process. If the *a priori* is reduced to the level of the *a posteriori*, it becomes impossible to base on the *a*

[1] *Eth.* iv. 3.

priori any beliefs that go beyond the range of subjective experience. If the self and the not-self are taken simply as different finite things, which we can observe in turn, their relations must be brought under the general laws of the connection of finite things with each other; and the phenomena of mind must be treated, like the phenomena of matter, as facts to be accounted for according to these laws.

But this of itself indicates a way of escape both from the introspective theory and from the empiricism to which it is opposed. For it suggests the question—What is the source of those very laws which guide the procedure of science in accounting for facts, psychological facts among others? When a scientific psychologist of the modern school attempts to show how, by habituation of the individual and the race, the necessity of thought expressed in the law of causation has been produced in the minds of the present generation of men, it is obvious that his whole investigation and argument presuppose the law whose genesis he is accounting for. A glaring instance of such circular reasoning is found in the writings of the most prominent representative of the school in the present day. Mr. Spencer begins by laying down as a first postulate of science that necessity of thought must be taken as a criterion of truth. It is by the continual aid of this postulate that he constructs his system of nature, and finally his psychological theory of the development of consciousness in man. Yet the main object of this psychological theory seems to be to account for the very necessities with which the author starts. Obviously such a philosophy contains elements of which the author is imperfectly conscious; for it involves that mind is not only the last product but the first presupposition of nature, or, in other words, that in mind nature returns upon its first principle. But to admit this is at once to lift the conscious being as such above the position which he would hold as merely a finite part of a finite world. It is to assert that nature has an essential relation to a consciousness which is developed in man, and that in the growth of this consciousness we have, not an evolution which is the result of the action of nature as a system of external causes *upon him*, but an evolution in which nature is really "coming to itself," *i.e.*, coming to self-consciousness, *in him*.

Now it was Kant who first—though with a certain limitation of aim—brought this idea of the relativity of thought and being to the consciousness of the modern world. In the *Critique of Pure Reason*, thought, indeed, is not set up as an absolute *prius*, in relation to which all existence must be conceived, but it is set up as the *prius* of experience, and so of all existences which are objects of our knowledge. Experience is for Kant essentially relative to the unity of the self; it exists through the necessary subsumption of the forms and matter of sense under the categories, as, on the other hand, the consciousness of self is recognised as essentially dependent on this process. On this view, the *a priori* and *a posteriori* factors of experience do not really exist apart as two separate portions of knowledge. If they are severed, each loses all its meaning. Perceptions in themselves are void; categories in themselves are empty. We do not look outwards for one kind of truth and inwards for another, nor do we even, by an external process, bring facts given as a contingent under principles recognised as necessary; but the *a priori* is the condition under which alone the *a posteriori* exists for us. Even if it is allowed that the facts of inner and outer experience contain a contingent element or matter, given under the conditions of time and space, yet neither time nor space nor the facts of experience conditioned by them exist for us, except as elements of an experience which is organised according to the categories.

This is the essential truth which Kant had to express. It is marred in his statement of it by the persistent influence of the abstract division between contingent matter given from without and necessary principles supplied from within, a division essentially inconsistent with the attempt to show that the contingent matter is necessarily subsumed under these principles, and indeed exists for us only as it is so subsumed. But Kant himself puts into our hands the means of correcting his own inadequacy, when he reduces the inaccessible "thing in itself," (which he at first speaks of as affecting our sensibility and so giving rise to the contingent matter of experience,) to a noumenon (νοούμενον) which is projected by reason itself. The *Dialectic* exhibits the idea of thought as not only constituting finite experience but also reaching beyond it, though as yet only in a negative way. The mind is, on this view, so far unlimited that it knows its own limits; it is conscious of the defects of its experience, of the contingency of its sensible matter, and the emptiness and finitude of its categories; and, by reason of this consciousness, it is always seeking in experience an ideal which it is impossible to realise there. Thought measures experience by its own nature, and finds experience wanting. It demands a kind of unity or identity in its objects which it is unable to find in the actual objects presented to it. It is this demand of reason which lifts man above a mere animal existence, and forces him by aid of the categories to determine the matter of sense as a world of objects; yet, as this finite world of experience can never satisfy the demand of reason, the consciousness of it is immediately combined with the consciousness of its limited and phenomenal character. The student of the *Critique of Pure Reason* cannot but recognise the strange balance between the real and the phenomenal in which it ends, allowing to man the consciousness of each so far as to enable him to see the defects of the other,—so that by aid of the pure identity of reason he can criticise and condemn the "blindness" or unresolved difference of experience, and by means of the concreteness and complexity of experience he can condemn the "empty" identity of reason.

In order, however, to understand the full bearing of Kant's criticism of knowledge, and at the same time to find the meeting-point of the opposite currents of thought which alternately prevail in it, it will be necessary to consider the subject a little more closely. The lesson of the *Critique* may be gathered up into two points. In the first place, it is a refutation of the ordinary view of experience, as something immediately given for thought and not constituted by it. In the second place, it is a demonstration of the merely phenomenal character of the objects of experience, *i.e.*, the demonstration that the objects of experience, even as determined by science, are not things in themselves. Both these results require to be kept clearly in view, if we would understand the movement of thought excited by Kant. On the one hand, Kant had to teach that what is ordinarily regarded as real, the world of experience, is transcendentally ideal, *i.e.*, is determined as real by *a priori* forms of thought. On the other hand, he had to teach that the world so determined is empirically and not transcendentally real, *i.e.*, its reality is merely phenomenal. With the former lesson he met the man of science, and compelled him to renounce his materialistic explanation of the world, as a thing which exists in independence of the mind that knows it. The world we know is a world which exists only as it exists *for us*, for the thinking subject; hence the thinking subject, the ego, cannot be taken as an object like other objects, an object the phenomena of which are to be explained like other phenomena by their place in the connexion of experience. Having, however, thus repelled scientific materialism by the proof that the reality of experience is ideal, Kant refuses to proceed to the complete identification of reality with ideality, and meets the claims of the metaphysician with the assertion that the reality of experience is merely phenomenal. Hence he rejects any idealism that would involve the negation of things in themselves beyond phenomena, or the identification of the objects of experience with these things. The reality we know is a reality which exists only for us as conscious subjects, but this, though it is the only reality we can know, is not the absolute reality.

It is, however, to be observed that the nature of this opposition, between phenomena and things in themselves, seems to change as we advance from the *Analytic*, where the existence of such things is presupposed, to the *Dialectic*, where the grounds of that presupposition are examined. At first the opposition seems to be between what is present in consciousness and what is absolutely beyond consciousness. The matter of experience is regarded as given externally in the affections of the sensible subject,—affections caused by an unknown thing in itself, of which, however, they can tell us nothing. On the other hand, the form of experience, the categories and principles of judgment which turn these affections into objects of knowledge, are not pure expressions of the real nature, the pure identity, of the subject in itself, but only products of the identity of the self in relation to the sensibility and its forms of time and space. Hence, on both sides we must regard experience as merely phenomenal, alike in relation to the noumenal object and in relation to the noumenal subject, which lurk behind the veil and send forth into experience, on the one side, affections which become objects through their determination by the unity of thought, and, on the other side, an identity of thought which becomes self-conscious in relation to the objects so determined by itself.

Kant, however, having thus answered the question of the possibility of experience by reference to two things in themselves which are out of experience, is obliged to ask himself how the *consciousness* of these two things in themselves, and the criticism of experience in relation to them, is possible. And here, obviously, the opposition can no longer be conceived as an opposition between that which is and that which is not *in* consciousness. For the things in themselves must be present to consciousness in some fashion, in order that they may be contrasted with the phenomena. If, therefore, phenomena are now regarded as unreal, it must be because we have an *idea of reality* to which the reality of experience does not fully correspond. In the *Analytic* Kant had been speaking as if the real consisted in something which is not present to the conscious subject at all, though we, by analysis of his experience, can refer to it as the cause of that which is so present. Now, in the *Dialectic*, he has to account for the fact that the conscious subject himself is able to transcend his experience, and to contrast the objects of it as phenomenal with things in themselves.

Now it is obvious that such an opposition is possible only so far as the thought, which constitutes experience, is at the same time conscious of itself in opposition to the experience it constitutes. The reason why experience is condemned as phenomenal is, therefore, not because it is that which exists for thought as opposed to that which does not exist for thought, but because it imperfectly corresponds to the determination of thought in itself. In other words, it is condemned as unreal, not because it is ideal, but because it is *imperfectly* ideal.[1] And the absolute reality is represented, not as that which exists without relation to thought, but as that which is identical with the thought for which it is. In the *Dialectic*, therefore, the noumenon is substituted for the thing in itself, and the noumenon is, as Kant tells us, the object as it exists for an intuitive

[1] Cf. *Critical Philosophy of Kant*, ii. p. 150 *seq.*

or perceptive understanding, *i.e.*, an understanding which does not synthetically combine the given matter of sense into objects by means of categories, but whose thought is one with the existence of the objects it knows. It is the idea of such a pure identity of knowing and being, as suggested by thought itself, which leads us to regard our actual empirical knowledge as imperfect, and its objects as not, in an absolute sense, *real* objects. The noumena are not, therefore, the unknown causes by whose action and reaction conscious experience is produced; they represent a unity of thought with itself to which it finds experience inadequate.

Now this higher unity of thought with itself is what Kant calls reason, and he identifies it with the faculty of syllogising. Hence the three forms of syllogism seem to him to point to three forms, in which the pure unity of reason presents itself to us in opposition to the merely *synthetic* unity of experience, a psychological, a cosmological, and a theological form. In each of these cases the empirical process of knowledge is accompanied, guided, and stimulated by an idea which nevertheless it is unable to realise or verify. In psychology, our investigations are prompted and regulated by an idea of the identity of the self, which is never realised in our actual self-consciousness, because the self of which we are conscious is manifold in its states, and because it stands in relation to an external world. The idea of simple identity is, therefore, something we may set before us as the goal of an ideal psychology, to which we may approximate, in so far as we can trace unity of faculty through all the differences of mental phenomena, but to which we can never attain, owing to the nature of the matter with which we deal. Again, in our scientific attempts to explain our external experience, the unity of reason takes the form of an idea of the world as a completed infinite whole, which contains all the objects known to us and all other possible objects; but this idea cannot be realised in an experience which is conditioned by space and time, and is, therefore, ever incomplete. The idea of totality is, therefore, an *ideal*, which guides and stimulates our scientific progress, without which such a thing as science could not exist, but which at the same time can never be realised by science. Lastly, the unity of reason takes a third form in which identity and totality are combined,—as the idea of a unity in which all differences, even the difference of subject and object, are transcended,—the idea of a unity of all things with each other and with the mind that knows them. This idea also is one which science can neither surrender nor realise. It cannot surrender it, without giving up that striving after unity without which science would not exist; and it cannot realise it, for the difference between the world, as it is presented to us in actual experience, and the subjective determination of our thinking consciousness, cannot be overcome. We can, indeed, use the idea that the world is an organic whole, determined in relation to an end which consciousness sets for itself, as an *heuristic* principle to guide us in following the connection of things with each other; but, as we cannot, by means of any such idea, anticipate what the facts of external experience will be, so we cannot prove that, for a mind other than ours, the unity of things which we represent in this way might not take a quite different aspect. Indeed we have reason to think it would; for, while we always think of a designing mind as using materials which have an existence and nature independent of the purposes to which they are put, the absolute mind must be conceived as creating the materials themselves, by the same act whereby they are determined to an end. We must conceive it, in short, as an intuitive understanding, for which end and means, objective and subjective, are one, or, in other words, as an intelligence whose consciousness of itself is or contains the existence of all that is object for it.

This new view of the things in themselves as *noumena* or ideals of reason involves a new attitude of thought towards them, different from that dogmatic attitude which is provisionally adopted in the *Analytic*. Accordingly, we now find Kant speaking of them, not as things which exist independently of their being conceived, but as "problematical conceptions" of which we cannot even determine whether they correspond to any objects at all. They are "limitative" notions which have a negative value, in so far as they keep open a vacant space beyond experience, but do not enable us to fill that space with any positive realities. They are like dark lanterns which cast light upon the empirical world, and show what are its boundaries, but leave their own nature in obscurity. All that we can say of the noumenal self or subject is, that it corresponds to the unity implied in all knowledge, but whether there is such a self, independent of the process of empirical synthesis and the self-consciousness which accompanies that process, we cannot tell. All that we can say of the noumenal reality of the objective world is, that it corresponds to the idea of the objects of experience as a completed whole in themselves apart from the process whereby we know them, but whether there is any such real world independent of the process of experience, it is impossible to say. Lastly, all that we can say of God is, that He corresponds to the idea of the unity of all things with the mind that knows them,—an ideal which is involved in all knowledge,—but whether the realisation of this idea in an intuitive understanding is even possible, we have no means of determining, however we may suspect that understanding and sensibility are "branches springing from the same unknown root." The *Criticism of Pure Reason* ends, therefore, in a kind of see-saw between two forms of consciousness—a thinking consciousness, which transcends experience and sets before us an idea of absolute reality, but which cannot attain to any knowledge or even certitude of any object corresponding to this idea, and an empirical consciousness, which gives us true knowledge of its objects, but whose objects are determined as merely phenomenal and not absolutely real.

The equipoise thus maintained between the empirical and the intelligible world is, however, in the *Critique of Practical Reason*, overbalanced in favour of the latter. What the theoretical reason could not do "in that it was weak through the flesh," through its dependence on the very empirical consciousness which it sought to transcend, is possible to the practical reason, because it is primarily determined by itself. In our moral consciousness we find ourselves under a law which calls upon us to *act* as beings who are absolutely self-determined or free, and which, therefore, assures us that our intelligible self is our real self, and conclusively determines our empirical self in contrast with it as phenomenal. Thus the moral law gives reality to the intelligible world; or, as Kant expresses it, "the idea of an intelligible world is a point of view beyond the phenomenal which the reason sees itself compelled to take up in order to think of itself as practical." In other words, the moral law presupposes freedom or self-determination in the rational being as such, and makes him regard himself, not merely as a link in the chain of conditioned existences in time and space, but as the original source of his own life. The blank space beyond the phenomenal thus begins to be filled up by the idea of a free causality, which in its turn postulates a world adequate and conformable to itself. And the man who, as an empiric individuality, is obliged to regard himself merely as an individual being, determined by other individual beings and things according to the law of necessity, is authorised as a moral being to treat this apparent necessity as having its reality in freedom, and to look upon himself as the denizen of a spiritual world, where nothing is determined for him from without which is not simply the expression of his own self-determination from within. "Thus we have found, what Aristotle could not find, a fixed point on which reason can set its lever, not in any present or future world, but in its own inner idea of freedom,—a point fixed for it by the immovable moral law, as a secure basis from which it can move the human will, in spite of the opposition of all the powers of nature."[1] Starting from this idea of freedom, therefore, Kant proceeds to reconstruct for *faith* the unseen world, which in the *Critique of Pure Reason* he had denied as an object of *knowledge*. Nor is he content to leave the two worlds in sharp antithesis to each other, but even in the *Critique of Practical Reason*, and still more in the *Critique of Judgment*, he brings them into relation to each other, and so gives to theoretical reason a kind of authority to use, for the explanation of the phenomenal world, those ideas which otherwise it would be compelled to regard as illusive.

In all this, however, it is difficult to avoid seeing a partial retractation of Kant's first view as to the irreconcilable opposition of the phenomenal and the noumenal. For, in the first place, the moral imperative is addressed to a self which is at one and the same time regarded in both characters, and which is called upon to subsume under the moral law actions which otherwise derive their character and meaning from the relations

[1] Kant, i. 638 (Rosenkranz' edition).

of the phenomenal world. That the particular nature of men as phenomenal individuals can be the means of realising the universal law of reason, is implied in all Kant's statements of the latter, and particularly in his conception of men as constituting together a "kingdom of ends"; for it is difficult to conceive this kingdom otherwise than as an organic unity of society, in which each individual, by reason of his special tendencies and capacities, has a definite office to fulfil in realising the universal principle that binds all the members of the kingdom to each other. The *Summum Bonum*, again, is said to consist in the union of happiness with goodness, *i.e.*, of the empirical conditions of man's individual life as a sensible subject with the pure self-determination of the intelligible self; and God is postulated as a *Deus ex machina* to bind together these two unrelated elements,—a conception which shows the difficulty into which Kant has brought himself by defining them as unrelated.

In the *Critique of Judgment* Kant makes a final effort to escape from the dualism involved in his original analysis of experience. For in that work he maintains that the consciousness of the beautiful and the sublime is or involves a harmony of the understanding or the reason with sense; and, what is still more important, he points out that the idea of organic unity, without which we cannot explain the phenomena of life, contains in it a possibility of the reconciliation of freedom and necessity, of the intelligible and the phenomenal. This idea, he argues, we are authorised by our moral consciousness to apply to the whole course of the things in the phenomenal world, and so to regard it as a process to realise the moral ideal. No doubt he again partially retracts this view, when he declares that we must treat the idea of final causality as a *subjective* principle of judgment, which is to be regarded as necessary not for all intelligence, but only for us as finite intelligences. But such saving clauses, in which Kant recurs to the dualism with which he started, cannot hide from us how near he has come to the renunciation of it.

When we regard Kant in this way as asserting from one point of view an absolute limit, which from another point of view he permits us to transcend, it becomes obvious that his philosophy is in an unstable equilibrium, which cannot but be disturbed by any one who attempts to develop or even to restate his ideas. Hence we need not wonder that those who take in earnest his denunciations of any attempt to transcend experience generally,—like Professor Huxley,—reject as worthless all Kant's later work; and that, on the other side, those who take in earnest his ideas of freedom, of organic unity, of an intuitive understanding, and of a *Summum Bonum* in which freedom and necessity meet together, are compelled to break through the arbitrary line which he drew between knowledge and belief. In favour of the former course it is easy in many places to appeal to the letter of Kant. In favour of the latter it need only be pointed out that, in Kant's view, all experience rests upon, or is in its development guided by, those ideas which yet he will not permit us to treat as sources of knowledge. Hence the principles of the *Critique* cannot legitimately be used against metaphysic, except by those who are prepared to admit the ideas of reason, up to the point to which he admits them, as ideas that limit and direct our experience,—while rejecting all use of them to cast light upon that which is beyond experience. In other words, those who would adopt his alternative must maintain the possibility of a purely negative knowledge, *i.e.*, the possibility of the knowledge of a limit by one who yet cannot go beyond it. They must show how it is possible for us to have an ideal of knowledge which enables us to criticise experience without enabling us to transform it; they must show how ideas of the supersensible can so far be present to our thought as to make visible the boundaries of the prison of sense in which we are confined, without in any way enabling us to escape from it.

Is this possible? We may gather up the Kantian antithesis in the assertion that experience is the imperfect realisation of an ideal of knowledge derived from reason, by means of materials derived from sense and understanding, the nature of which is such that they can never be brought into correspondence with the ideal. But this ideal, in all its three forms, as we have seen, is simply the idea of a pure unity or identity in which all differences are lost or dissolved—whether they be differences in inner or differences in outer experience, or, finally, the differences between the inner and the outer, the subjective and the objective.

Kant's view therefore is, in effect, this: that thought carries with it the consciousness of an identity or unity, to which our actual experience in none of its forms fully corresponds. On the other hand, Kant does not hesitate, with equal emphasis, to condemn the identity of thought as "empty" and subjective, because it does not contain in itself nor can evolve from itself the complex matter of experience. But this alternate condemnation of experience as unreal from the point of view of the ideas, and of the ideas as unreal from the point of view of experience, seems to show that *both* are unreal, as being abstract elements, which have no value save in their relation to each other, and which lose all their meaning when separated from the unity to which they belong. According to this view, ideas and experience, noumena and phenomena, if they are opposed, are also necessarily related to each other. If our empirical consciousness of the world of objects in space and time, as determined by the categories, does not correspond to the unity or identity of thought which is our ideal of knowledge, yet that idea of unity or identity is set up by thought in *relation* to experience, and cannot, therefore, be essentially irreconcilable with it. The two terms may be opposed, but their opposition cannot be absolute, seeing that they are in essential relation to each other. It is a great logical error not to discern that a negative relation is still a relation, *i.e.*, that it has a positive unity beyond it. This positive unity may not, indeed, be consciously present to us in our immediate apprehension of the relation in question, but is necessarily implied in it. Now it is just because, in his separation of noumena and phenomena, Kant omits to note their essential relativity, that he is forced to regard the former as a set of abstract identities of which nothing can be known, and the latter as the imperfect products of a synthesis which can never be completed or brought to a final unity. Yet the value of his whole treatment of the ideas of reason in relation to our intellectual and moral experience arises from the fact that, in practice, he does not hold to this abstract separation of the two elements. Ideas absolutely incommensurable with experience could neither stimulate nor guide our empirical synthesis; they could not even be brought into any connection with it. When, therefore, Kant brings them into this connection, he necessarily alters their meaning. Hence the pure abstract identity which excludes all difference is changed in its application into the idea of an organic unity, of which the highest type is found in self-consciousness with its transparent difference of the subjective and objective self. It would be absurd and meaningless to say that science seeks to reduce experience to an abstract identity, in which there is no difference, unless for this were tacitly substituted what is really an entirely different proposition, that science seeks to find in the infinitely diversified world of space and time that unity in difference of which self-consciousness has in itself the pattern. It is in reference to the former kind of identity—the abstract oneness of formal logic—that Kant proves that it is impossible for experience to be made adequate to ideas. But it is only of the latter kind of identity—the oneness of self-consciousness—that it can be said that it furnishes a guiding principle to scientific investigation or an ideal of knowledge.

The same confusion is still more evident in Kant's account of our moral experience, in dealing with which he directly attempts to get synthetic propositions out of the pure identity of reason, in other words, to draw definite moral laws out of the logical principle of non-contradiction. Whatever success he attains is gained by substituting for the formal principle of *self-consistency* the positive idea of *consistency with the self*, and again by conceiving this self as a concrete individual, the member of a society, and so standing in essential relation to other selves. The pure abstraction from all the external results of action and from all motives of desire, which at the beginning of the *Metaphysic of Ethics* Kant declares to be essential to morality, is modified and indeed transformed, as we go on, by the admissions that other rational beings are *not* external to us in any sense that excludes their good from being an end of our endeavour, and that the desires are *not* irrational and immoral except in so far as they are directed to the pleasures of the sensuous individual (which in a conscious being they never entirely are). Both in the speculative and in the practical sphere, therefore, the absolute opposition of the ideal or noumenal to the empirical disappears, as soon as

Kant attempts to apply it. For, in both, the abstract identity of formal logic, which is really the meaning of the noumenon as absolutely opposed to, and incommensurable with experience, gives way to the unity of self-consciousness,—a unity which is so far from being *absolutely* opposed to the difference of the empirical consciousness that it necessarily implies it. For self-consciousness presupposes the consciousness of objects, and though it is opposed to that consciousness, it is essentially correlated with it; hence its opposition to it cannot be regarded as absolute, or incapable of being transcended.

These considerations may throw some light on the relation of the *Analytic* and *Dialectic* of Kant, and on the nature of the opposition of noumenon and phenomenon as it is presented in the latter. In the deduction of the categories, Kant pointed out the essential relation of the objective world of experience to what he called the "transcendental unity of apperception"; *i.e.*, he pointed out that the unity of consciousness is implied in all its objects. This unity, he further showed, must be conceived as "capable of self-consciousness"; but it actually becomes conscious of self only in relation, though also in opposition, to the other objects determined by it. Now it is this consciousness of itself in opposition to other objects which is the source of Kant's "ideas of reason," of the dissatisfaction of the mind with its empirical knowledge, even in its scientific form, and of the demand for a higher kind of knowledge to which experience is not adequate. That a standard is set up for experience by which it is condemned, is simply a result of the further development of that unity which is implied in experience—a result of the progress of thought from consciousness to self-consciousness, and of the contrast between the former and the latter. The problem with which Kant's *Dialectic* attempts to deal, and which it treats as insoluble, is, therefore, simply the problem of *raising consciousness to the form of self-consciousness;* in other words, of attaining to a knowledge of the world of experience as not merely a "synthetic," and therefore imperfect, unity of things external to each other, but as an organic unity of transparent differences, a self-differentiating, self-integrating unity, such as seems to be presented to us in pure self-consciousness. Nor can this problem be regarded as insoluble;

for the unity of self-consciousness is identical with the unity of consciousness; it is only that unity become self-conscious. Hence the point of view at which consciousness and self-consciousness seem to be absolutely opposed to each other,—the highest point of view which Kant *distinctly* reaches,—can be regarded only as a stage of transition from the point at which their relative difference and opposition is not yet developed, to the point at which they are seen to be the factors or elements of a still higher unity.

The later philosophy of Germany, from Kant to Hegel, is little more than the development of the idea just stated in its twofold aspect. In the first place, it is an attempt to show what is involved in the idea of thought or self-consciousness as in itself an organic whole, a many-in-one, a unity which expresses itself in difference, yet so that the difference remains transparent, and therefore is immediately recognised as expression of the unity. In the second place, it is an attempt to bridge over the difference between thought or self-consciousness and the external world of experience, and to show that this opposition also is subordinated to a higher unity. Or, to put it more directly, the idealistic philosophy of Germany seeks, on the one hand, to develop a logic or metaphysic which bases itself, not, like formal logic, on the idea of bare identity, but on the idea of self-consciousness; and, on the other hand, to show, in a philosophy of nature and spirit, how, by means of this logic, the opposition of thought to its object, or of the *a priori* to the *a posteriori* in knowledge, may be transcended. In the third and fourth sections of this article something more will be said of the manner in which this task was fulfilled. Here only a few words are necessary to sum up the results reached, and to give more distinctness to the new ideal of knowledge which those results suggest.

We have seen that Kant's critical attitude involved two things,—on the one hand, the assertion that the existence we know is necessarily existence for thought, and, on the other hand, the denial that that which exists for our thought is absolute reality, a denial which again involves the presence to our thought of an ideal of knowledge, by which our actual knowledge is condemned. This ideal, however, was falsely conceived by Kant as an identity without any difference, and, in this sense, he does not hesitate to apply it even to self-consciousness itself. For, in a remarkable passage,[1] he attempts to prove that the consciousness of self is not a knowledge of the self, by a simple reference to the duality of the self knowing and the self known, arguing that the ego "stands in its own way," just because it exists only *for itself*, *i.e.*, because in knowing itself it presupposes itself. Kant evidently thinks that to know the real self it would be necessary to apprehend it in simple identity, as purely an object without reference to a subject, or purely a subject without reference to an object. Yet to this it seems sufficient to answer that such an object or subject would lose its character as object or subject, and would become equivalent to mere being in general; and that, as being in general is a mere abstraction, to know it cannot be the ideal of knowledge. If therefore there be a unity or identity of thought which is not realised in experience, and in reference to which we can regard experience as an imperfect form of knowledge, it cannot be found in this abstract identity of being. In truth, as we have seen, it

[1] *Kritik*, p. 279 (Rosenkranz' edition), cf. Hegel, v. p. 258.

is found in that very idea of self-consciousness which Kant is criticising. Just because we are self-conscious, and therefore oppose the unity of the conscious self to the manifoldness of the world in space and time, do we seek *in* the world of space and time for a transparent unity which we cannot at first find there. But, when this is seen, we find in Kant himself the partial solution of the difficulty. Self-consciousness presupposes consciousness; for, while the apprehension of objects in consciousness is possible only in relation to the unity of the self, yet it is only in relation to and distinction from these objects that we are conscious of that unity. Hence the two opposites, self and not-self, are bound together, and presuppose a unity which reveals itself in their opposition, and which, when made explicit, must reconcile them. If, therefore, self-consciousness, in its first opposition to consciousness, gives rise to an ideal of knowledge to which our empirical knowledge of objects is inadequate, this arises from the fact that not only empirical knowledge, but also the ideal to which it is opposed, is imperfect, or that they both point to a unity which is manifested in their difference, and which is capable of containing and resolving it. In other words, the opposition of science to its ideal, which Kant has stated in his *Antinomies*, is not an absolute opposition, but one the origin and end of which can be seen.

This opposition reaches its highest point in the contrast between the transparent unity of self-consciousness, in which the difference of knower and known is evanescent, and the essential manifoldness and self-externality of the world in space, in which the differences seem to be insoluble. We must, indeed, think of self-consciousness as having life in itself and therefore as differentiating itself from itself; but this differentiation is held within the limit of its unity, it is a separation of movements which are separated only as they are united. On the other hand, the world in space presents itself as the sphere of external determination, in which things are primarily disunited and act only as they are acted on from without, and in which this external influence never goes so far as to destroy their reciprocal externality. In this sense it is that the opposition of mind and matter was taken by Des Cartes, and it is a survival of the same mode of thought that leads many even now to draw absolute lines of division between *a priori* and *a posteriori*, between ideas and facts, between spiritual and natural. Kant and Fichte give a new aspect to the difficulty by showing that the difficulty is one of reconciling consciousness and self-consciousness, and that in consciousness there is already present the unity which is manifested in self-consciousness, as, on the other hand, it is only through consciousness and in opposition to it that self-consciousness is possible. And Fichte made a further step when he attempted to show that the categories and the forms of perception, time and space, which Kant had taken as inexplicable facts, are implied in this contrast of consciousness and self-consciousness. The error that clings to Fichte's speculations is, however, that he treats consciousness merely as a necessary illusion which exists simply with a view to self-consciousness, and hence is led to regard self-consciousness itself—because it is essentially related to this necessary illusion—as a schema or image of an unknowable absolute. In fact, in the end Fichte falls back upon the abstract identity in which Kant had found his noumenon, and his philosophy seems to lose itself in mysticism. Even

Schelling, though he saw that the absolute unity must be one that transcends the difference of self and not-self, did not finally escape the tendency to merge all difference in absolute oneness. On the other hand, it was the endeavour of Hegel to proceed in the opposite way,—not to lose self-consciousness or subjectivity in a mere unity of substance, but rather to show that the absolute substance can be truly defined only as a self-conscious subject. And just because he did this, he was prepared to take a further step, and to regard the external world, not as Fichte regarded it, as merely the opposite of spirit, nor as Schelling regarded it, as merely the repetition and co-equal of spirit, but rather as its necessary manifestation, or as that in and through which alone it can realise itself. His doctrine therefore might be summed up in two propositions,—first, that the absolute substance is spiritual or self-conscious, and, secondly, that the absolute subject or spirit can be conceived as realising itself only through that very world of externality which at first appears as its opposite. In both respects Hegel's philosophy reverses the *via negativa* of mysticism, and teaches that it is only through the exhaustion of difference that the unity of science, of which the mind contains in itself the certitude, is to be realised. For mind or spirit, viewed in itself, is conceived as a self-differentiating unity, a unity which exists only through opposition of itself to itself. And it is but a necessary result of such a conception that spirit can fully realise its unity only through a world which in the first instance must present itself as the extreme opposite of spirit. Hence the process of thought in itself, which is exhibited in the logic, ends in the opposition to thought of a world which is its negative counterpart. And the "absolute spirit" of Hegel is thus, not pure self-consciousness, but that more concrete unity of self-consciousness with itself which it attains through and by means of this world.

The effect of this view upon the relation of metaphysic to science, which we are at present considering, is noticeable. It does not, as is often supposed, supersede science by an *a priori* construction of the universe, nor does it leave the results of science unchanged and simply provide for it a deeper foundation. The latter was the point at which Kant and Fichte stopped; for, while they showed the relativity of experience to the principle of self-consciousness, they conceived that the function of metaphysic is completed in showing the phenomenal character of the objects of science, and in reserving a free space beyond the phenomenal world for "God, freedom, and immortality." Schelling, on the other hand, as he did not adopt this merely negative view of the relation of spirit to nature or of *a priori* to empirical truth, was obliged to reinterpret the latter by the former. As, however, he did not recognise any distinctions which were not merely quantitative, he was led to apply the same easy key to every lock, and to think that he had explained all the different forms of existence, organic and inorganic, when he had merely pointed out a certain analogy between them. The metaphysic of Hegel, whatever may be said of the actual philosophy of nature produced by its author, contains no necessity for any such arbitrary procedure. In his *Logic*, indeed, he attempts to give us *in abstracto* the movement of thought in itself, from its simplest determination of being as qualitative or quantitative, through the reflective categories of substance and cause, up to its full consciousness of itself in its organic unity. And in so doing he of course gives us an account of the various categories which science uses in the interpretation of nature.[1] He further attempts to show that the highest categories of science are in themselves imperfect and self-contradictory,—in other words, that they mark a stage of thought which falls short of that unity of being and knowing after which science is striving, and which is the presupposition as well as the goal of all intelligence. But, while he does this, he clearly acknowledges two things,—in the first place, that nature is essentially different from pure self-consciousness, and that therefore logic can never by direct evolution of its categories anticipate the investigations of science; and, in the second place, that the final interpretation of nature through the highest categories presupposes its interpretation by the lower categories, and cannot be directly achieved without it. In other words, science must first determine the laws of nature according to the principles of causality and reciprocity, ere philosophy can be in a position to discover the ultimate meaning of

[1] This subject—the progress of thought from lower to higher categories and methods—will be more fully discussed in the third section.

nature by the aid of higher principles. "The philosophy of nature," says Hegel, "takes up the material, which physical science by direct dealing with experience has prepared for it, at the point to which science has brought it, and again transforms this formed material without going back to experience to verify it. Science must, therefore, work into the hands of philosophy, in order that philosophy in its turn may translate the lower universality of the understanding realised by science into the higher universality of reason, and may show how in the light of this higher universality the intelligible world takes the aspect of a whole which has its necessity in itself. The philosophic way of looking at things is not a capricious attempt, once in a way for a change, to walk upon one's head after one has got tired of walking upon one's feet, or to transform one's work-a-day face by painting it over; but, *it is because the scientific manner of knowing does not satisfy the whole demand of intelligence, philosophy must supplement it by another manner of knowing.*" [1]

The result then may be briefly expressed thus. Kant and his successors showed the relativity of

[1] Hegel, vii. p 18.

the object of knowledge to the knowing mind. He thus pointed out that the ordinary consciousness, and even science, are abstract and imperfect modes of knowing, in so far as in their determination of objects they take no account of a factor which is always present, to wit, the knowing subject. For *their* purposes, indeed, this abstraction is justifiable and necessary, for by it they are enabled within their prescribed limits to give a more complete view of these objects in their relation to each other, than if the attempt had been made to regard them also in relation to the knowing subject. At the same time the scientific result so arrived at is imperfect and incomplete, and it has to be reconsidered in the light of a philosophy which retracts this provisional abstraction. For it must be remembered that the fact that science looks at things only in their relation to each other, and not to the knowing mind, narrows the points of view or categories under which it is able to regard them, or, in other words, limits the questions which the mind is able to put to nature. Just because science does not treat its objects as essentially related to the mind, it is unable to rise to what Hegel calls the point of view of reason, or of the "*Begriff*"; *i.e.*, it is obliged to treat objects and their relations under a set of categories, the highest of which are those of causality and reciprocity, and it is incapable of attaining to the conception of their organic unity. In other words, it is able to reach only a *synthetic* unity of *given* differences, and it cannot discover a principle of unity out of which the differences spring and to which they return. Now philosophy goes beyond science just because, along with the idea of the relativity of things to the mind, it brings in the conception of such a unity. Its highest aim is, therefore, not merely, as Kant still held, to secure a place for the supersensible beyond the region of experience. It is to reinterpret experience, in the light of a unity which is presupposed in it, but which cannot be made conscious or explicit until the relation of experience to the thinking self is seen,—the unity of all things with each other and with the mind that knows them.

2. *Relation of Metaphysic to Psychology.*—It has already been shown that the doctrine that the thinking subject is presupposed in all objects of knowledge—or, in other words, that existence

means existence for a conscious self—is not to be taken in a psychological sense. The idea that all science is based on psychology, and that, therefore, metaphysic and pyschology are identical, cannot be retained by any one who has entered into the full meaning of the Kantian criticism. It is, however, so natural a misinterpretation of it, and it is so much favoured by the letter of the very book in which it was first decisively refuted, that it will be useful to point out more directly the fallacy involved in it, especially as this will place us in a better position to determine the true relation of the two parts of philosophy thus confounded.

The misunderstanding first took a definite form in the introduction to Locke's *Essay*, in which he proposes to provide against any undue application of the intellectual powers of man to problems which are too high for them, by first examining and measuring the powers themselves. Stated in this way, it is obvious that the proposal involves an absurdity; for we have nothing to measure with, except the very powers that are to be measured. To see round our knowledge and find its boundary, we must stand outside of it, and where is such a standing ground to be found?

We cannot by knowing prescribe limits to knowledge, or, if we seem to be able to do so, it can only be because we compare our actual knowledge with some idea of knowledge which we presuppose. In this way the ancient Sceptics—and modern writers like Sir W. Hamilton and Mr. Spencer who have followed them—turned the duality involved in the idea of knowledge against its unity, and argued that because we cannot know the object except as different from and related to the subject, we cannot know it as it is in itself. Obviously in this argument it is involved that, in true or absolute knowledge, the object must not be distinguished at all from the subject,—to which the easy answer is that *without* such distinction knowledge would be impossible. The sceptic argument, therefore, lands us in the unhappy case of the German proverb: "If water chokes us, what shall we drink?" The object cannot be known if it *is* distinguished from the subject, and it cannot be known if it is *not* distinguished from the subject. Obviously the one objection is as good as the other, and both combined only show that the idea of knowledge involves distinction as well as unity, and unity as well as distinction.

The sceptic insists on one of these characteristics to the exclusion of the other, and condemns our actual knowledge because it contains both. In Kant there is undoubtedly some trace of the same fallacy, in so far as the idea, by contrast with which he condemns the objects of experience as phenomenal, is the idea of an abstract identity without any difference; but we have seen that with him this abstract identity is on the point of passing into an altogether different idea—the idea of self-consciousness as the type of knowledge.

It appears, then, that the idea of measuring our powers before we employ them rests on a paralogism; for it really means that we isolate one of the elements of the idea of knowledge, and then condemn knowledge for having other elements in it. It is possible to criticise and condemn special conceptions as not conforming to our idea of knowledge; but it is not possible to criticise the idea of knowledge itself; all we can do is to explain it. It is possible to see the limited and hypothetical character of certain of our ideas or explanations of things, because we are conscious that in developing them we have left out of account certain of the elements which are necessary to the whole truth; but this criticism itself implies, as the standard to which we appeal, the consciousness of truth and reality, a consciousness which we cannot further criticise. Here, therefore, we come upon what must seem, to all who think it admissible to question the very possibility of knowledge, an inevitable reasoning in a circle. We can answer objections only by means of the very idea which they dispute. But the answer is nevertheless a good one; for the objector also stands within the very circle which he seeks to break, and has no means of breaking it except itself. As soon as he speaks he can be refuted by his own words; for his doubts also presuppose that unity of the intelligence and the intelligible world which he pretends to deny.

The error, however, cannot be fully corrected until we consider what it is that gives it plausibility. The confusion of the metaphysical with the psychological problem is due to the fact that the being who is the subject of knowledge, for whom all exists that does exist, appears to be one, and only one, of the many objects of knowledge. When we say that existence means only an existence for a thinking self, we seem to be identifying the whole world with the feelings and ideas of men, *i.e.*, with certain phenomena that belong to the life of a class of beings which only forms a part of that world,—phenomena, moreover, that are not exactly the same in any two of that class of beings. If we are to escape this difficulty, it is obvious that we must be able to separate the conscious self or subject, as it is implied in all knowledge, from the nature of man as a being who "though formally self-conscious" is yet "part of this partial world," *i.e.*, one of the objects which we know along with and in distinction from other objects, and in whom "the self-consciousness which is in itself complete, and which in its completeness includes the world as its object," is only progressively realised.[1] Metaphysic has to deal with conditions of the knowable, and hence with self-consciousness as that unity which is implied in all that is and is known. Psychology has to inquire how this self-consciousness is realised or developed in man, in whom the consciousness of

[1] Green's General Introduction to Hume's *Treatise on Human Nature*, § 152. Works, i. 131.

self grows with the consciousness of a world in space and time, of which he individually is only a part, and only to parts of which he stands in immediate relation. In considering the former question, we are considering the sphere within which all knowledge and all objects of knowledge are contained. In considering the latter, we are selecting one particular object or class of objects within this sphere,—although no doubt it must make a great difference in our treatment of this object that we have to consider it as existing not only for us but for itself. If nature " becomes self-conscious in man," it is impossible to treat man *merely* as one among the other objects of nature. But it is not less true that he *is* one of those objects, and, in this point of view, the department of science or philosophy that deals with his life is as distinct from metaphysic —which deals with the conditions of all knowing and being—as is astronomy or physics. In both cases we have before us objects which we may consider in themselves, apart from their relations to the conscious subject; and in both cases we must take cognisance of these relations, if we would have a complete and final view of those objects. It is possible to have a purely objective psychology, *i.e.*, a psychology which abstracts from the relation of man to the mind that knows him, just as it is possible to have a purely objective science of nature. Such a natural science of man, however, will necessarily abstract at the same time from the fact, that in man there is manifested that universal principle, in relation to which all things are and are known. In other words, it will omit that distinctive characteristic of man's being, in virtue of which he is a subject of knowledge and a moral agent. Hence the abstraction in this case is more likely to lead to positive error, more likely to produce not only an imperfect but a distorted view of the object. Inorganic nature, if we take it *in itself*, is not untruly viewed, under the categories of causality and reciprocity, as a collection of objects externally determined by each other; the error lies only in taking it as if it could exist in itself. Even organic beings do not suffer much injustice in being brought under such categories; for, though, as living and still more as sensitive beings, they involve, in themselves and in their relation to the world, a kind of unity of differences to which the categories of external relation imperfectly correspond, yet they are not such unities *for themselves*, but only *for us*. In other words, the principle, through which they are and are known, is still external to them. Hence also they are determined by outward influences, though these influences act rather as stimuli to what we may call the self-determined movement of their own life than as mechanical or chemical forces which change it. But in man, in so far as he is self-conscious,—and it is self-consciousness that makes him man,—the unity through which all things are and are known is manifested; and therefore he is emancipated, or at least is continually emancipating himself, from the law of external influence. Nature and necessity exist for him as that from which his life starts, in relation to which he becomes conscious of himself, against which he has to assert himself, and in the complete overcoming of which lies the end of all his endeavour. Nature is the negative rather than the positive starting-point of his existence, the presupposition against which he reacts rather than on which he proceeds; and, therefore, to treat him simply as a natural being is even more inaccurate and misleading than to forget or deny his relation to nature altogether. A true psychology must, however, avoid both errors; it must conceive man as at once spiritual and natural; it must find a reconciliation of freedom and necessity. It must face all the difficulties involved in the conception of the absolute principle of self-consciousness,—through which all things are and are known,—as manifesting itself in the life of a being like man, who "comes to himself" only by a long process of development out of the unconsciousness of a merely animal existence.

This problem first presented itself in a distinct form in the discussions of the Socratic school as to the nature of knowledge, discussions which turned mainly upon the relation of the conscious to the unconscious element in thought. Socrates, by his method more than by any direct statement, drew attention to the fact that all particular judgments in morals involve or presuppose a universal principle. At the same time he pointed out that, so far from this universal principle being known to those who are continually making such judgments, they are not even conscious of its existence. They constantly use general terms whose meaning they have never even thought of defining. The beginning of a rational life for them must therefore lie in their becoming conscious of their ignorance, *i.e.*, conscious that they have been all along judging, and therefore acting, on untested and even unknown assumptions. They must bring the unconscious universal to the light of day and define it, for until that is done, it is impossible to live a moral, that is, a rational life. "Virtue is knowledge," *i.e.*, it is acting, not according to opinions, or particular judgments, judgments whose universal is unknown, and which therefore may be regarded as expressing merely the impulses or habits of the individual, but in view of a universal principle determined by reason.

The one-sidedness of this view—which absolutely condemns as vice all virtue that is not based on conscious principle—was partly corrected by another part of the doctrine of Socrates, who taught that knowledge is something that must be evolved from within the mind, and not merely communicated to it from without. For this implies that the moral principle may be present in men's minds, and may rule their thoughts and actions, long before they become directly conscious of it. They are rational although they have never thought about reason, and they do not wait for scientific ethics to judge and act morally, any more than they wait for logic to reason correctly. It is this line of thought which is universalised and mythically expressed by Plato in his doctrine of "reminiscence." According to this myth, we were conscious of ideas or universals in our pre-natal state; we forgot them in the shock of birth into this mortal life; but in feeling or sharing the rapture of the poet or the lover we recall them, as identified or confused with particular objects which "are like them, or partake in them." The same explanation is given of the practical skill of the general and the statesman, and even of the "right opinion" which guides the ordinary good man.[1] Such opinion is neither knowledge nor ignorance: not knowledge, for in it general principles or ideas are not present to the mind *as* ideas, and therefore the particular objects cannot be distinctly subsumed under them; yet not ignorance, for the ideas are after all present, though wrapped up in the particulars or confused with them. Nay, in the *Theætetus*, Plato endeavours to show that the

[1] *Meno.* 99 C.

pure particular without the universal, sensations without ideas, cannot enter into our consciousness at all, and that therefore the lowest point to which a conscious being can descend is "opinion," in which particular and universal, sensible and intelligible, are mingled together. In other words, no conscious being can apprehend the particular except through the universal, though that universal may be present only *in* consciousness and not *to* it. The task of philosophy is therefore only to make men "recollect" themselves, *i.e.*, to make *self-conscious* that universality of thought in which all rational beings "partake," or which, in the language of later philosophy, constitutes reason. The imperfection of Plato's view lay, however, in this, that, while he clearly recognised that the condition of all consciousness of the particular is the universal, he did not see with equal clearness that the universal has a meaning only in relation to the particular. And this tendency to separate universal from particular is naturally accompanied by a tendency to set the subjective against the objective, and to regard the world, not as the manifestation of reason, but as a dualistic world, in which reason is chained to a lower principle

—a world which can at best only give a hint or suggestion to the mind which may enable it to "recollect" itself and recover for itself its own treasures. Thus the false method of introspection, the "high *priori* road" of mysticism, was at least opened up by Plato, if he did not himself altogether forsake the narrower and harder way to the spiritual world through nature and experience.

The great step in advance taken by Aristotle was due to his seeing the danger of this tendency. Those, however, who have maintained that Aristotle is the great *a posteriori* philosopher, as Plato is the great *a priori* philosopher, have entirely mistaken the bearing of Aristotle's criticism of the Platonic theory. As strongly as Plato does Aristotle maintain that reason is δυνάμει πάντα τὰ νοητά, and that, therefore, the apprehension of truth *by* the mind is not a mere external communication of it *to* the mind, but rather is the mind coming to a consciousness of itself. As firmly as Plato does he declare that truth in its highest form is self-evidencing, *i.e.*, that the principles of science, the laws of nature, when once they have been discovered, are seen to be true by their own light. His statements to this effect have been neglected or explained away, because they were supposed to be inconsistent with his still more frequently reiterated assertions that it is only from experience and by induction that the truth of things can be discovered. Writers of a later day,—who came to Aristotle with an idea of a fixed opposition between *a priori* and *a posteriori*, and who held that the only possible alternatives were *either* to divide knowledge between the two *or* to explain away one of them,—could not comprehend that Aristotle might be in earnest *both* in asserting that knowledge is derived from experience, *and* in asserting that it is an apprehension by reason of that which is identical with itself and needs no extraneous evidence. But Aristotle started with no such fixed opposition. On the contrary, any one who reads the last chapter of the *Posterior Analytics* will see that he had no difficulty in maintaining that knowledge begins in the apprehension of τὸ καθ' ἕκαστον in sense perception, and that it proceeds from many perceptions to experience, and from many experiences to science ; while at the same time he declared that the principles of science have their evidence in themselves. And the meaning of this declaration is shown in the *De Anima*, where we find him speaking of knowledge as the realisation in the "passive reason" of man of an "active reason" which is eternal and unchangeable, and which in the consciousness of itself includes the knowledge of all things. Of this realisation, indeed, there is in man only the potentiality or capacity, but just because this is a pure or universal capacity, because, as Aristotle puts it, it has no quality or determination of its own to stand between it and its objects, it is a capacity in which the absolute reason can realise itself, a capacity of knowing all things.[1] Here we have Plato's myth of reminiscence freed from the metaphor of memory, and reduced to scientific terms; for that myth simply meant that the evolution of knowledge is the development of the mind to that consciousness of itself, and of all that is potentially in it. Only, by the combination of this doctrine with the idea of the necessity of induction, Aristotle guards against the purely subjective interpretation to which in Plato it was liable. For the process by which the mind "comes to itself" is conceived as a process by

[1] *De Anima*, iii. ch. 4.

which at the same time it rises from the particular. to the universal, from the γνώριμα ἡμῖν to the γνώριμα ἁπλῶς, from the bare apprehension of the facts of experience to the knowledge of them through their principles or laws.

Yet Aristotle was as little able as Plato to work out fully a theory of the relation between the universal and the individual reason; and the cause of this failure was in both cases substantially the same. In Plato's philosophy, the ideal tended to divorce itself from the phenomenal world in such wise that the latter was regarded only as suggesting or partaking in the former, but not as entirely explicable by it. It was not merely that, to the mind of the individual in its progress, the veil was only gradually lifted from the rationality of the world, but that in the world there was an irrational element from which the mind could save itself only by flight into the region of abstraction. And, though Aristotle by his doctrine of the essential relation of ideas to experience, or of the development of the mind to the acquisition of knowledge of the world, seemed to be on the way to correct this error, yet he too shrinks from regarding the phenomenal world as in itself intelligible. To him also an irrational matter mingles with things, and is in them a source of contingency and imperfection. Chance is not merely the reflection upon the world of our imperfect knowledge, but a fact of experience, and there is therefore a region in which our best science cannot rise above generality to universality. In this way there remains for Aristotle an absolute *a posteriori*, a reality which cannot be understood, and which we can scarcely conceive as existing at all for the divine intelligence. At this point the Aristotelian philosophy appears to stand between two alternatives; *either* that, in the sense of pantheism, the finite world and its contingency is an illusion, *or* that it is contingent only for the growing intelligence of man, which fully understands neither itself nor the world which is its object. Aristotle, however, does not choose either horn of the dilemma, and leaves us therefore with an unresolved dualism between thought and its object; and this again necessarily involves a dualism between the active reason, which, as he asserts, realises itself in man, and the passive reason which constitutes his nature as a finite being.

In the Middle Ages the Platonic and Aristotelian idea that the apprehension of objective truth is one with the evolution of the mind to self-consciousness seemed to be entirely lost. Knowledge of the finite world was regarded as of little value, and knowledge of the infinite was conceived to be something given on authority, and in reference to which the mind was confined to an attitude of passive reception or implicit faith. No greater slavery of the spirit can be conceived than that in which even the truths of religion and morality —the truths that regard the inmost life of the spirit itself—were taken as a lesson to be learned by rote from the lips of a teacher. Yet the consciousness that such truth, if it was to be received by the mind, still more if it was to transform the mind, could not be entirely foreign to it, found a voice in the scholastic philosophy. And the compromise or truce between faith and reason expressed in the saying of Anselm *credo ut intelligam,*—according to which reason was to confine itself to the analysis and demonstration of the data received in implicit faith from the Church, —prepared the way for the recognition that the two are not essentially at variance. The mind that proceeds from *veneratio* to *delectatio*, from awe and submission to the doctrine to enjoyment and appreciation of it, must already in its awe and submission have the beginnings of an intelligent appreciation. Anselm's saying might be understood simply as meaning that we must have spiritual experience, ere we can understand the things of the spirit. And in this sense it was adopted by the Reformers to express an idea almost the opposite of that with which the Scholastics had associated it, —the idea that the direct apprehension of spiritual truth as entering into the inner life of the subject, as identified with his very consciousness of self, is the basis of all knowledge of it. In the Protestant church of the period after the Reformation, we find a growing tendency to insist on the subjectivity of religion, in the same exclusive and one-sided way in which the mediæval Church had insisted on its objectivity. In some extreme representatives of Protestantism this went so far as to lead to a disregard, almost to a rejection, of all objective doctrine, and a reduction of theology to an account of the religious consciousness. On the other hand, while religion was thus made subjective, science claimed to be purely objective, and the followers of Bacon seemed to adopt towards nature the same attitude of passive receptivity which the mediæval Christian was taught to hold towards the Church. While man was to learn everything from himself in religion, he was to learn nothing from himself in science. His aim must be to exclude subjective *idola*, in other words, to accept the facts as they were given, and keep himself out of the way. The inevitable result of this difference of view as to the nature of knowledge in these two different regions was, however, on the one hand a withdrawal of religion from all connection with finite interests, and, especially from the attempt to connect religious principles with the knowledge of the finite world, and, on the other hand, an increasing tendency in those who represented finite science to regard religion as something merely subjective and even individual, as a feeling which could not be translated into thought or made the basis of any knowledge of the objective world.

The opposite principles of certitude, which were thus set up for religious truth and truth of science, need only to be brought together and contrasted to betray that they rest upon opposite abstractions, neither of which expresses the complete nature of truth or knowledge. On the one hand the truths of religion were maintained just because they were not, or were not merely, *objective*, but were capable of being tested by inner experience, and identified with the self-consciousness of the individual. On the other hand the truths of science were maintained because they were not, or were not merely, *subjective*, but were capable of being verified in objective experience. It was rightly seen on the one side that mere subjective feelings or opinions have no validity for any one but the subject of them, and on the other side that what is merely objective or externally given can have permanent value and interest for the intelligence only as it ceases to be mere isolated and unrelated fact—nay, that, even when science has discovered law and order in nature, its results still want the highest value and interest so long as that law and order are not seen as standing in essential relation to the intelligence itself. The idea of truth or knowledge as that which is at once objective and subjective, as the unity of things with the mind that knows them, enables us to understand the condemnation which the religious mind passed upon a merely external dogma, and even its lack of interest in a science which presented itself as an account of merely objective or external facts. And it enables us also to understand the way in which scientific men insisted upon objective fact as the basis of all knowledge, and the disrespect which they felt for a religion which seemed to admit that it had no such support. What is wanted to clear up the confusion on both sides is the growth of the perception among *scientific* men, that the objectivity which they are seeking cannot be mere objectivity (which would be unmeaning), but an objectivity that stands in essential relation to the intelligence, and, on the other hand, the growth of the perception among *religious* men, that the subjectivity of religion only means that God, who is the objective principle by whom things are and are known, is a spiritual Being, and can therefore be revealed to the spirit. When these two corrections have been made, it must become obvious that the religious consciousness is not the consciousness of another object than that which is present in finite experience and science, but simply a higher way of knowing the same object. And in this it is also involved that the two ideas of *a priori* and *a posteriori*, of that which is evolved from within and that which is given from without, are not essentially opposed to each other, but that the *a posteriori* is simply the first form of a consciousness which in its ultimate development must become *a priori*.

In that philosophy of compromise which was initiated by Descartes, one part of knowledge was regarded as innate, or developed from within, and another part as empirical, or imparted from without. In the second period of the history of modern philosophy this compromise was broken, and the names of Locke and Leibniz—though with some hesitation on both sides—represent respectively the theory that all knowledge is *a posteriori* and the theory that all knowledge is *a priori*. The compromise seemed to be renewed with Kant, but the form in which it was renewed pointed, as has been already shown, to something more than a compromise; for his doctrine was that the *a posteriori* element, the facts, exist for us only under *a priori* conditions, or, in other words, that what is usually called *a posteriori* is in part *a priori*. The criticism of this view need not be repeated. It is sufficient here to say that if, as Kant shows, the elements are inseparable or organically united, it is impossible to allege that so much belongs to the one and so much to the other. Furthermore, the consciousness of an essential difference in the elements of knowledge is possible, only so far as that difference is transcended by the unity of knowledge. We can distinguish the *a priori* from the *a posteriori* only on condition that we can transcend the distinction, and this means that the distinction itself is not absolute, but that there is a point of view from which the *a posteriori* may be regarded as *a priori*, and that which is given from without to the spirit may be referred to its own self-determined development.

Now it is just here that we come upon the great turning-point of philosophical controversy, in the form which it has taken in modern times. The problem may be expressed thus—In what sense can we apply the idea of development to the human spirit? Are we to treat that development as merely a determination from without, or as an evolution from within, or as partly the one and partly the other? In a sense all writers of the present day would admit that this last is the case.

For, on the one hand, even the Darwinian theory accounts for development by aid of what we may call the *a priori* tendency of the individual to maintain itself in the struggle for existence, though it supposes that the condition or medium in which the individual is placed determines the direction in which that development proceeds. And, on the other hand, no one now would adopt the Leibnizian theory that the individual is a monad, whose self-development is entirely conditioned by itself in such a sense that all the relations which it has to other existences are merely apparent, and that the coincidence of its life with the life of the world is the result of a pre-established harmony. On both sides, therefore, it would be admitted that in some sense the individual is determined by itself, though the tendency of the Darwinians would be to regard such self-determination as something merely formal; and on both sides it would also be admitted that self-determination does not exclude a determination from without, though extreme opponents of Darwin might be inclined to reduce this determination to a mere stimulus, or external condition, of the development of the nature of the subject to which the stimulus is applied.

The question, however, remains whether, after all, this opposition of without and within is an absolute one, or whether there is any point of view from which it may be transcended. To Aristotle it seemed possible to answer this question in the affirmative, because he conceived that the reason of man is a pure or universal δύναμις, the evolution of which to complete self-consciousness is one with the process whereby the objective world comes to be known. Yet, as Aristotle admitted the existence in the world of a material principle which was essentially different from the ideal principle of reason, he was obliged to limit his assertion of the possible unity of the subjective and the objective consciousness, and to say merely that "in things *without matter* the knower is identical with the known."[1] But this would immediately lead to the conclusion that the pure development of reason must be secured by abstraction from all finite and material objects, rather than by a thorough comprehension of them. The freedom of the spirit, on this theory, must be a negative and not a positive freedom, a freedom won, not by overcoming the world, but by withdrawing ourselves from its influence.

[1] *De Anima*, iii. 4.

It remained, therefore, for modern philosophy to work out the Aristotelian idea that the rational being as such, in spite of its necessary relation to and dependence on an external world, is never in an absolute sense externally determined. And, as we have already seen, the Kantian philosophy brought this problem within the reach of solution, in so far as it showed, first, that objective existence can have no meaning except existence for a thinking self, and, secondly, that existence for a thinking self means an existence the consciousness of which is "capable of being combined with the consciousness of self." Add to these propositions the doctrine which was maintained by Kant's successors, that *that* only can be combined with the consciousness of self which is essentially related to it, and we arrive at an idealistic theory of the world, which enables us at once to understand the relative value of the distinction between self-determination and determination from without, and at the same time to see that it is *only* relative. If it be true that nothing exists which is not a possible object of consciousness, and again that there is no possible object of consciousness which is not essentially related to the unity of the self, then the phenomena of the external world, which at first present themselves under the aspect of contingent facts, must be capable of being ultimately recognised as the manifestation of reason; and the history of the conscious being in his relations with that world is not a struggle between two independent and unrelated forces, but the evolution by antagonism of one spiritual principle. It is, on this view, the same life, which within us is striving for development, and which without us conditions that development. And the reason why the two terms, the self and the not-self, thus appear to be independent of each other, or to be brought together only as they externally act or react upon each other, lies in this, that the object is imperfectly known, and the subject is imperfectly self-conscious. This, however, does not make it less true that in self-consciousness is to be found the principle in reference to which the whole process may be explained, and therefore that the self-conscious subject, as such, lives a life which belongs to him, not merely as one object among others, but as having in himself the principle from which the life and being of all proceeds.

From this point of view, as has been already

indicated, the relative value of a theory of human development, such as that which might be based on the ideas of Darwin, would not be denied. The conscious being may be regarded simply as an externally determined object, and the incorrectness of this assumption will not entirely destroy the value of the results attained; especially if, as is often the case with those who seek to construct a natural science of man, the assumption itself is not very strictly adhered to, but corrected by the tacit admission of other conceptions somewhat inconsistent with it. But, at the same time, it would require to be pointed out that such a science is necessarily abstract and imperfect, as it omits from its view the central fact in the life of the object of which it treats. It can do nothing to account for man's consciousness, or his capacity of becoming conscious, of the influences by which he is supposed to be determined; or, to put it from the other side, it takes for granted that the objects that influence man are intelligible objects, "capable of being combined with the consciousness of self," without seeing how much is involved in this assumption. Now it is evident that the consciousness of an influence cannot be explained by the influence itself, nor even by that influence taken together with the nature of the sensitive beings subjected to it. It is evident also that an influence mediated by consciousness is not, strictly speaking, an external influence, but that it is already transformed, and in process of being further transformed, by the development of the self to which it is present. For the dawn of consciousness, in which the external object first comes into existence for us as opposed to the self, is at the same time the beginning of the process by which its externality is negated or overcome. Self-consciousness is that which makes us individuals in a sense in which individuality can be predicated of none but a self-conscious being. For, in determining himself as a self, the individual at the same time excludes from himself every other thing and being, and determines them as external objects. He emancipates himself from the world at the same time that he repels the world from himself. Yet this movement of thought, by which his individuality is constituted, is also that by which he is lifted above mere individuality, for, in becoming conscious of self and not-self in their opposition and relation, he ceases to be simply identified with the one to the exclusion of the other.

His finite individuality is regarded by him from a universal point of view, in which it has no less and no more importance than any other individuality, or in which its greater or less importance is determined only by its place in the whole. On this universality of consciousness rests the possibility of science and of morality. For all science is just a contemplation of the world *in ordine ad universum* and not *in ordine ad individuum*; and all morality is just action with a view to an interest which belongs to the agent, not as this individual, but as a member of a greater whole, and ultimately of the absolute whole in which all men and all things are included.

In this nature of the conscious subject lies also the possibility of metaphysic in the sense of Aristotle, as that science which goes *back* to a πρῶτον φύσει, a beginning which is prior to the existence in consciousness of the individual self, and *forward* to an end in which the divisions of the finite consciousness are transcended,—as including, in short, ontology, or metaphysic in the narrower sense, on the one side, and theology, or the philosophy of religion, on the other. In truth, these two extremes of science are necessarily bound together:

we cannot go back to the beginning, unless we can go on to the end; we can recover the first unity only if we can anticipate the last. Or, to free this thought from the associations of time, we cannot apprehend the unity which is involved or presupposed in all the differences of our conscious life, except in so far as we can look at our individual existence from the point of view of the whole to which it belongs.

This will become more evident, if we consider the nature of the limits which have to be transcended by such a science. The individual conscious subject, as he finds himself at first, is but one being in a world that stretches out, apparently without limits, on every side of him. Of the things by which he is immediately surrounded he sees but a small part, and the influences which he receives from them are, as he knows, like the wave that breaks upon a shore from an unknown ocean, only the last partial expression of impulses that come from regions beyond his ken. Again, he finds himself as one in a changing series of beings, of which he knows only the last preceding terms, and he is aware that in a few years he, as one of this series, will cease to be. He is thus to himself a definitely limited being, and though his knowledge of himself and his world may be gradually widened so as to reach some little way back into the past, and anticipate a little of the future, or may go outwards in space to embrace a widening circle of existences around him, yet he always stops at a limit, of which he is conscious that it is no absolute limit, but simply an arbitrary halting-place where vision grows indistinct and imperfect. When he reflects upon himself from this point of view, he is forced to regard himself as but a fragment, and a fragment of an unknown whole, by which his whole being is determined to be what it is. His highest knowledge seems to be but a consciousness of his ignorance, his highest freedom a determination by motives the ultimate meaning of which is hid from him.

So far there seems to be no room for any metaphysical knowledge, any knowledge of ourselves and our world, which is other than relative and *in ordine ad individuum*. But further reflection shows that in this very consciousness of limit there is implied a consciousness of that which is beyond limit. While we proceed from part to part, beginning with ourselves and our immediate surroundings, and following out lines of connection that lose themselves in the distance, we are guided by a consciousness of the whole as a unity through which the parts are determined. Nay, it is just the presence of this consciousness that makes us capable of what seems the piecework of our knowledge, in which, by the aid of the principle of causality, we connect particular with particular, and so gradually extend the sphere of light into the encompassing darkness. For that principle simply means that the limited external object does not sufficiently explain to us its own existence, and that therefore we are forced to explain it by a reference to something beyond it. It means, in other words, that we cannot rest in that which is not a self-bounded, self-determined whole. The application of the category of external determination has therefore an essential reference to the higher category of self-determination. The mere endlessness of space and time has no meaning except in opposition, yet in relation, to the true infinity, of which we find the type in self-conscious thought. Or, to put it in the Kantian form in which it is already familiar to us, the consciousness of the objective world in space and time stands in relation to the unity of self-consciousness. And if, when we regard the former exclusively, we are forced to view ourselves as insignificant and short-sighted finite beings in an infinite universe, when we regard the latter we are enabled to see that what is revealed in all that universe is only that spiritual principle which we find also in ourselves. In this way a new light is thrown on our first consciousness of ignorance. The strivings of our reason after knowledge can no longer be regarded as strivings after an unknown goal, but rather after a goal which it has prescribed for itself. The narrow limits of our individual life are not removed, but they cease to be for us the limits of a narrow circle of definition within a formless infinite. They become the limits of a sphere within a sphere, a sphere which is defined by the idea of knowledge or self-consciousness itself, and in which therefore, however we may wander, we are everywhere at home. In religious language, the sphere is not a mere universe, but God, who is without us only as He is within us, so that " by the God within we can understand the God without."

Again, as this consciousness takes man beyond his immediate existence, and enables him to determine it in relation to an absolute unity of all things in God, so it enables him to go back to a unity which is behind or prior to that existence. For, if the individual can look at himself just as he looks at others, and at others as he looks at himself, *i.e.*, if he can regard the world from a point of view which is unaffected by his individuality, and in which that individuality is for him only what it is for impartial reason, he can have nothing in him which binds his consciousness to his individuality as mere individuality. As therefore he can go beyond himself to apprehend the whole in which his individuality has a place, so there is nothing to prevent him from going back upon himself, and upon the conditions which are prior to his own individual being. He is not tied to his immediate life, and can go below it just as he can rise above it.

"O God, I think Thy thoughts after Thee," said Kepler. In reading the "thoughts" written in the planetary system, Kepler was discovering the meaning of that which is simpler and more elementary than the existence of man, as a cycle of mechanical relations is simpler and more elementary than self-consciousness. Yet it was a true feeling that led him to connect this descent into the mechanical world with God. For it is only in virtue of the same faculty which enables us to rise to the absolute life which includes and subordinates our own, that we can so free ourselves from the image of our own conscious life as to apprehend and comprehend the simpler relations of purely physical existence. But the same faculty of going back upon ourselves has a still deeper manifestation. Not only can we abstract from ourselves so as to understand the inorganic world, we can also abstract from ourselves so as to understand the conditions which are prior to the thought, and therefore to the existence, of any objective external world at all, the universal conditions of the knowable and therefore also of reality. In doing so, to use Hegel's metaphor, which is but an extension of Kepler's, we are "thinking what God thought and was before the creation of the world," *i.e.*, we are thinking the spiritual unity presupposed in all knowledge, and therefore in all objects of knowledge—the consciousness in relation to which everything is, and is known.

3. *The Relation of Metaphysic to Logic.*—The ordinary view of logic is based on two presuppositions which tend to separate it almost entirely from metaphysic: it is based on the presupposition of an opposition, or at least a merely external relation, between thought and its object, and again of an opposition, or merely external relation, between the form or method and the content or matter of thought. The intelligence is regarded as dealing with an object which is given to it externally, and which, therefore, it can truly represent, only if it leaves it unchanged and introduces into it nothing of its own. Truth, to use a well-known definition, is the agreement of our conceptions with their objects, and in bringing about this agreement all the concessions must be on the side of thought. Conformably to this view, the processes of thought must be purely analytic; *i.e.*, thought may break up the given idea of the object into its constituent elements, and again out of these elements it may recompose the idea in its unity, but it can add nothing and take nothing away. It is like an instrument which alternately dissects a solid mass

into smaller parts and again mechanically presses them together, but which never penetrates and dissolves the harder matter, still less fuses it into a new form, by bringing it into contact with new chemical elements.

This conception, like much of the philosophy of which it is a specimen, is a kind of exaggerated caricature of one aspect of the philosophy of Aristotle. Aristotle is the great analytic philosopher. He first laid down boundaries in that continuous domain of science which Plato had first surveyed. Not that he ever completely lost sight of the unity or continuity of the different sciences which he thus distinguished. His unrivalled genius is shown nowhere more clearly than in those not unfrequent utterances, weighty with speculative insight into the unity of things, in which, at a stroke, he makes his own landmarks and all landmarks to disappear. Yet such utterances generally stand by themselves, and do not alter the general analytic spirit of his philosophy. They are not so developed as to show distinctly the merely relative character of the divisions and distinctions which he elsewhere sets up, or the limits of the sphere within which they hold good. Hence it was easy for minds, which possessed something of Aristotle's keenness of understanding without his speculative depth, to neglect such expressions, or to explain them away. And this process of degradation was the more rapid, as the philosophy of Aristotle soon ceased to be studied in his own writings, and became a traditionary possession of the schools. In this way we may partly explain how logic came to be regarded by mediæval philosophy as a mere form of thought, which could be altogether separated from the matter, and by the application of which that matter could be in no way affected or changed. But for such a view, indeed, it is difficult to conceive how the schoolmen could have ventured to apply any logical processes at all to the sacred matter of dogma. The idea of externally adding anything to the faith once delivered to the saints was excluded by the principle of authority; and the idea of developing out of that faith anything that was not immediately contained in it had not yet presented itself to any one. Hence the business of thought seemed to be purely formal and analytic, and it was only on the plea of its being such, that its activity could be tolerated at all.

Nor was this view of logic at once changed by the revolt against scholasticism. The first philosophical exponents of the modern scientific movement, while they rejected the matter of dogma as fictitious, or at least as transcending the sphere of positive knowledge, and while they substituted in its place, as the object of investigation, the facts of experience, did not realise any more than the schoolmen that the form or method of knowledge could be other than analytic of given matter. Bacon, their protagonist, was above all solicitous to guard against any subjective *anticipatio naturæ;* nor did he see that the questions which, in his theory of "forms," he proposed that science should ask of nature, themselves involved any preconceived theory regarding it. Conscious, as every true scientific mind must be, that the study of nature involves a constant self-abnegation, a patient self-distrustful course of experiment and observation, he and his followers did not realise the presuppositions that make the inquiry possible, and by which it must be guided. Still less did they recognise that the separation between the mind and its object, which they took for granted, can only be a relative division, *i.c.,* a division on the basis of a unity, and that therefore the self-abnegation of the mind in its investigation of facts cannot be an absolute self-abnegation, but is only the first step on the way to the discovery that the facts are intelligible, and so essentially related to the intelligence. Hence to them logic still seemed an analytic process, the end and aim of which was understood to be that a world, existing in itself *out of* relation to thought, should be reproduced in a more or less imperfect image *in* thought. And, when it came to be suspected by a less naive philosophy of experience that, after all, certain presuppositions, not given in experience itself, were involved in the scientific interpretation of it, various expedients were devised to reduce these presuppositions in an indirect way to empirical truths,—expedients of which Mill's attempt to base the law of causality upon an *inductio per enumerationem simplicem* may be taken as the type.

When we go back to Aristotle,—who was the "founder of logic" in the sense that he was the first who treated logical method as a separate branch of science,—we find that his division of logic from metaphysic is by no means so definite and complete as it was made by some of his successors. The vindication of the highest principle of thought, the law of contradiction, is treated by him as the business of metaphysic. And, though he separates the idea of truth from the idea of reality, and regards the former as involving a relation of thought to a reality which is determined in itself independent of thought, yet he does not regard this independence as by any means absolute. Truth is defined by him as a connection or distinction of ideas which *corresponds* to a union or separation of things, but does not necessarily so correspond. This definition, however, holds good only in so far as things not essentially related are brought together κατὰ συμβεβηκός. Where necessity comes in, and is apprehended by reason, the case is different. For in that case we have not merely an external synthesis, but an essential identity, *i.e.*, a unity of elements which can neither be, nor be known, apart from each other. In relation to the principles of science, therefore, Aristotle holds that error, *i.e.*, a connection of ideas not corresponding to a connection of things, is impossible, and that the only alternatives are knowledge and ignorance. Either we possess the idea or we do not possess it; as Aristotle otherwise expresses it, in thought we are either in contact with the things or not in contact with them; there is no third possibility. The meaning of Aristotle becomes clearer when we remember that, according to his view, the intelligence, in apprehending the indivisible unity of elements in the object, is at the same time apprehending the unity of the object with itself. The mind cannot be deceived in regard to that which forms a part of its consciousness of itself. In freeing the essential conception of the object from the contingency of matter, science has freed the object from that which made it foreign to the intelligence, and the relation of thought to things ceases to be one of correspondence, and becomes one of identity.

The legitimate inference from this view of the relation of the intelligence to the intelligible world would seem to be, that the partial separation of thought from its object, and its imperfect correspondence with it, are characteristic of our first empirical consciousness of things, and of the stage in which we are advancing from that consciousness to science, but that in completed science the division ceases. The *esse* of things is not their *percipi*, but their *intelligi*. But, if this be taken as the truth, then it can no longer be supposed that the process by which scientific knowledge is attained, consists simply in an analysis of the object as it is given in immediate perception. On the contrary, it must be held that, if our thought has to submit itself to the object, and if it has to be brought into conformity with the object by a process of induction, it is equally true that in this process the object also must be changed, that it may be brought into conformity with the principle of thought. The genesis of science, according to this view, is not merely an analysis of given facts, but a process of vital transformation, by which consciousness on the one side and the object on the other are brought into unity with each other. The idea, indeed, of an empty process, a process in which the activity of the mind is merely formal, is one which will not stand the slightest examination. A mind without categories, if such a thing were conceivable, would have no questions to ask in relation to the object presented to it, and could therefore get no answers. Those who make a pretence of approaching an object in an absolutely receptive attitude, and without any presuppositions, only show that they are unconscious of the categories by which their thought is ruled; and they will be most slavishly guided by these categories just because they are unconscious of them. The schoolmen, indeed, when they applied their logical principles to the matter of Christian dogma, did not recognise that they were doing more than analysing and bringing out clearly the meaning of that dogma. But the effect of their work was to turn the whole system of theology into a collection of insoluble puzzles; for the doctrine they had to analyse was a doctrine of reconciliation between divine and human, infinite and finite, universal and particular, and the principle of their method was to treat all these oppositions as absolute. In like manner it might be shown that the analysis of social phenomena which was made in the last century, was inadequate and superficial, just because of the latent assumption of individualism on which it proceeded, and that the greater success of writers like Comte and Spencer does not arise, merely or mainly, from their being more careful observers of the phenomena of social life, but in great part from the fact that, rather by the unconscious movement of opinion than by any distinct metaphysic, their minds have become possessed by more adequate categories.

The idea that the process of thought is merely formal, or analytic of given matter, is, however, an error that has a truth underlying it. This is the truth expressed by Aristotle in his much misunderstood comparison of the intelligence of man to a *tabula rasa*, upon which nothing at first is written, and again in his assertion—already quoted—that the mind is a pure δύναμις, without any distinguishing quality of its own which could prevent it from apprehending the real nature of other things. For the meaning of these statements is that self-conscious reason is not a special thing in the world, but the principle through which all things are, and are understood; and that, therefore, prior to experience, the undeveloped reason of man is undetermined and indifferent, and open to be determined in one way or another, according to the object to which it is directed. Hence the conscious subject, as such, is not bound to his own individuality, but can regard things, nay, in a sense, must regard them, from a point of view which is independent of it. This is what makes possible the self-restraint and self-abnegation prescribed to the scientific man, whose whole duty, as it is often said, is to keep himself out of the way and let the objects speak, to lay aside all subjective *idola* and prejudices that stand between him and the reality of things.. This at first sight may seem to be equivalent to the assertion that the mind ought to be in a state of simple passivity or receptivity towards objects. What is really meant, however, is not that the intelligence should go out of itself, or cease to be itself, that it may know its object, but simply that it should show itself in its universality, or freedom from the limits of the individual nature. The self-abnegation of science is an endeavour, so to speak, to see the object with its own eyes, but this it can do only in so far as the consciousness, for which the object is, is that consciousness in relation to which alone all objects are, and are understood. Or, to put this in another form, the conscious self in its scientific self-abnegation does not give itself up to another, and become purely passive; it only gives up all activity which is not the activity of that universal thought, for which and through which all things are. Hence, when it has so abnegated itself, its most intense constructive activity is just beginning, though, just so far as the self-abnegation has been real, that constructive activity has become one with the self-revelation of the object. As, however, it is only through the constructive activity of thought that there exists for us any object at all, so it is only through its continued activity that the conception of the object is changed, till it is completely revealed and known. And this activity involves a continuous synthesis, by which an ever wider range of facts is brought together in an ever more definite unity, until the mind has, if we may use the expression, exhausted its store of categories upon the world, and until the world has completely revealed itself in its unity with itself and with the mind.

To combine these two ideas—on the one hand that science begins in a self-abnegation by which the mind renounces all subjective prejudices and thereby attains a purely objective attitude, and on the other hand that this purely objective attitude is not a mere attitude of reception, but one in which the mind is continually transforming the object by its own categories,—to see that the universality of the mind in knowing is not mere emptiness, and that its activity is synthetic just when it is most free from all pre-suppositions extraneous to the nature of its object,—is one of the greatest difficulties of the student of metaphysic. Universality at first looks so *like* emptiness, and a universal activity so *like* a merely formal activity, that it is no wonder that the one should be mistaken for the other. But if we make such a confusion, we may soon be forced to choose between a sensationalism that makes knowledge impossible and a mysticism that makes it empty. For this the pure identity of thought with itself, which is involved in the process of analysis, is put on the one side, and the manifold matter of experience, which is the object of thought, on the other, and between these opposites no mediation is possible. If we take our stand upon the latter, we are forced to reject all mental synthesis as invalid, because it involves a subjective addition to the facts; if we take our stand on the former, we are compelled to regard all objective experience as irrational, because it does not correspond to the pure identity of thought.

In Aristotle's view of logic it cannot be said that this difficulty is clearly solved, though he seems to have seen the error of both extremes. On the one hand, he often recognises the synthetic character of the process of induction, as when he speaks of the universal idea or law as a central principle, in which we must find the key to all the difficulties suggested by different aspects of a given subject. Yet in other places we trace the influence of a merely analytic conception of that process, as a process in which the universal is to be reached by abstracting from the peculiarities of individuals. And this conception of it is favoured by Aristotle's metaphysical theory, according to which the forms of things in the finite world are manifested in a resisting matter, a matter which prevents them from being perfectly or universally realised. For, in so far as this is the case, the facts will not be entirely explained by the knowledge of the form, and the knowledge of the form must be obtained, not by combining all the facts, but rather by abstracting from them. Again, in Aristotle's account of the process of thought in the *Prior Analytics*, he regards it as a formal deductive process; and, though in the *Posterior Analytics* he attempts to give a synthetic meaning to the syllogism,—by treating it as the process in which the properties of a thing may be proved of it, or combined with it, through its essential definition,—yet this adventitious meaning bestowed upon the syllogistic process does not alter its essential nature.

Now the ultimate source of this inadequate view of the process of thought seems to lie in Aristotle's imperfect conception of the unity or identity which is for him the type of knowledge. For though, both in the *Metaphysic* and the *De Anima*, he defines that identity as a self-consciousness or as a consciousness of objects which is identical with self-consciousness, yet he does not seem clearly to distinguish between a unity in which there is no difference, and a unity in which difference is transcended and reconciled. This seems to be shown by his description of the principles which reason apprehends as *individua* or indivisible unities, rather than unities which imply, while they transcend, difference. Yet, in the definition of the unity of knowledge as self-consciousness, Aristotle has implicitly admitted that there is a duality or difference in the unity itself, and this might have been expected to modify his conception of the relation of consciousness to its objects. For, as self-consciousness is not simple like a chemical element, but only in the sense that it is an indissoluble unity of opposites, it might have been anticipated that one, who had realised self-consciousness as the principle of knowledge, would be able to regard the opposition between the consciousness of self and the consciousness of the world as itself also capable of being conceived as a unity.

This misconception of Aristotle may be shown in another way. In the *Metaphysic* we find him laying down what is called the logical law of contradiction as the ultimate principle of knowledge. The meaning of this principle, however, as Aristotle states it, is simply that thought in its essence is definition or distinction. If, as Heraclitus says, everything at once is and is not, if we cannot attach any definite predicates to things by which they may be distinguished from each other, then, Aristotle argues, thought is chaos, and knowledge is impossible. If determination be not negation, if the assertion of A be not the negation of not-A, then there is no meaning in words. The criticism to be made on this view is obviously, not that it is a false statement of the law of thought, but that it is an imperfect statement of it. Thought is undoubtedly *distinction;* and, if all distinction be confounded, no meaning can be apprehended or expressed. But thought is also *relation*; or, in other words, it connects together the things which it distinguishes: and this aspect of it is equally important with the other. Aristotle shows his one-sidedness — a one-sidedness which throws him into opposition to Plato, but which enables him to correct Plato only by falling into the opposite error—when he exclusively fixes his attention on the "differentiating" aspect of knowledge, and takes no notice of the "integrating" aspect of it. It is easy to see that this exclusive attention to one side of the truth may lead in many ways to a distorted view, both of the world and of the intelligence that apprehends it. If Heraclitus be interpreted as simply denying the right of thought to introduce its definiteness into the flux of sense, nothing but absolute scepticism can come out of his philosophy; and Aristotle was right in maintaining that it is only as the flux is brought to a stand, and the universal is fixed as a permanent and definite object of thought,[1]

[1] ἠρεμήσαντος τοῦ καθόλου ἐν τῇ ψυχῇ, *An. Post.* ii. 19.

that knowledge becomes possible. But, on the other hand, if distinction be taken as absolute, if the definite assertion of a thing be taken as a negation of all relation to what it is not, if the fixity of thought be treated as an abstract self-identity, which excludes all the movement of finite things,—wherein they show their finitude and pass beyond themselves into other things,—then knowledge will be equally impossible. Our consciousness, on such a theory, would be disintegrated into parts, which would own no connection with each other; nor would it be possible for us to think of things as, in spite of their differences, bound together into the unity of one world. The law of contradiction or distinction, therefore, is likely to lead to serious misconceptions, unless it be complemented by a *law of relation*—a law expressing the truth that there is a unity which transcends all distinction. For all intelligible distinction—all distinction of things in the intelligible world—must be subordinate to their unity, as belonging to that world, and therefore essentially connected with each other and with the intelligence. In such a world, in other words, there can be no *absolute* distinctions or differences (not even between being and not-being); for distinction without relation is impossible, and a conception held in absolute isolation from all correlated conceptions ceases to have any meaning. This does not, of course, imply a negation of the law of contradiction within its own sphere, but it does imply that that sphere is limited, and that there is no absolute contradiction. All opposition is within a pre-supposed unity, and therefore points to a higher reconciliation, a reconciliation which is reached when we show that the opposition is one of correlative elements.

The great step in logical theory which was taken by the idealistic philosophy of the post-Kantian period, was simply to dissipate the confusion which had prevailed so long between that bare or formal identity, which is but the beginning of thought and knowledge, and that concrete unity of differences, which is its highest idea and end. It was, in other words, to correct and complete the two imperfect conceptions of thought, as analytical, and as externally synthetical, by the conception of it as self-determining, to show that it is a unity which manifests itself in difference and opposition, yet through all the antagonism into which it enters, is really developing and revealing its unity with itself. This new movement of thought might, in one point of view, be described as the addition of a third logic to the logic of analysis and the logic of inductive synthesis, which were already in existence. But it was really more than this; for the new logic was not merely an external addition to the old logics, but it also put a new meaning into these logics, by bringing to light the principles that were involved in them. At the same time it broke down the division that had been supposed to exist between logic and metaphysic, between the form or method of thought and its matter. It showed that thought itself contains a matter from which it cannot be separated, and that it is only by reason of this matter that it is able to ask intelligent questions of nature, and to get from nature intelligible answers. A short space must be devoted to explain this relation of the three logics to each other.

The *analytic logic* fairly represents our first scientific attitude to the world, in which we concentrate our attention upon the facts as they are given in experience, with no thought of any mental synthesis through which they are given. To ourselves, in this stage of consciousness, we seem to have to do with an object which is altogether independent of our thought, and what we need in order to know it, is only to keep ourselves in a purely receptive attitude. All we can do is to analyse what is given, without adding to it anything of our own. It has, however, already been pointed out that this apparent self-abnegation is possible only because, in abnegating our individual point of view, we do not abnegate the point of view which belongs to us as universal or thinking subjects. In other words, the objectivity of knowledge thus attained is not the ceasing of the activity of our thought, but rather of all that interferes with that activity. We seem to abstract from ourselves, but what we do abstract from is only the individuality that stands between us and the world. The scientific observer who has thus denied himself, however, is not necessarily conscious of the meaning of what he has done. The immediate expression of his consciousness is not "I think the object," but "it, the object, *is*"; and the more intensely active he is, the more his activity is lost for him in the object of it. His whole work is, for himself, only the analysis of given facts, and beyond that he seems to have nothing to do but to take the world as he finds it. The voice of nature to which he listens, is for him not his own voice but the voice of a stranger; nor does it occur to him to reflect that nature could not speak to any one but a conscious self. His business is to determine things as they present themselves, to enumerate their qualities, to measure their quantities; and his logic therefore is a logic governed by the idea of the relative comprehension and extension of the things which he thus names and classifies. Such an analytic logic seems to be all that is necessary, because the only predicates by which things are as yet determined are those which are involved in their presence to us in perception, and as perceived they seem to be at once given in all their reality to the mind that apprehends them.

A step is taken beyond this first naive consciousness of things, whenever a distinction is made between appearance and reality, or whenever it is seen that the things perceived are essentially related to each other, and that therefore they cannot be known by their immediate presence to sense, but only by a mind which relates that which *is*, to that which *is not*, immediately perceived. If "the shows of things are least themselves," we must go beyond the shows in order to know them; we must seek out the permanent for that which is given as transient, the law for the phenomenon, the cause for the effect. The process of thought in knowledge therefore is no longer lost in its immediate object, but is, partly at least, distinguished from it. For, just in proportion as the reality is separated from the appearance, does the knower become conscious of an activity of his own thought in determining things. From this point of view nature is no longer an object which spontaneously reveals itself to us, but rather one which hides its meaning from us and out of which we must wring its secret by persistent questioning. And, as this questioning process obviously has not its direction determined purely by the object itself, it becomes manifest that the mind must bring with it the categories by which it seeks to make nature intelligible. To ask for the causes of things, or the laws of things, presupposes that their immediate appearance does not correspond to an idea of reality which the mind brings with it, and by which it judges that appearance. Nature is supposed to be given to or perceived by us as a multitude of objects in space passing through successive changes in time; and what science seeks is to discover a necessity of connection running through all this apparently contingent coexistence and succession, and binding it into a system. Science, therefore, seems to question nature by means of an idea of the necessary interdependence and connection of all things, as parts of one systematic whole governed by general laws—an idea which it does not get from nature, but which it brings to nature. Hence the logic in which this process of investigation expresses its consciousness of itself will be a *synthetic logic*, a logic built on certain principles which are conceived to be independent of experience, and by the aid of which we may so transform that experience, so penetrate into it or get beyond it, as to find for it a better explanation than that which it immediately gives of itself. The *Posterior Analytic*, in which Aristotle brings in the idea of cause to vivify the syllogistic process, or supply a real meaning to it, may already be regarded as a first essay in this direction. And the theory of inductive logic, as explained by Bacon, Mill, and their successors, is a continuous attempt to determine what are the principles and methods on which experience must be questioned, in order to extract from it a knowledge which is not given in immediate perception.

It was, however, Hume who first brought into a clear light the subjectivity of the principles postulated in this logic, and especially of the principle of causality, which is the most important of them. In thus contrasting the subjectivity of the principles of science with the objectivity of the facts to which they are applied, it was his intention to cast doubt on science in so far as it is based on the application of the former to the latter. The principles, he maintained, are not legitimately derived from the facts, therefore they cannot legitimately be used to interpret them. They are due to the influence of habit, which by an illegitimate process raises frequency of occurrence into the universality and necessity of law, and so changes a mere subjective association of ideas into an assured belief and expectation of objective facts. The answer given by Kant to this sceptical criticism of science involved a rejection of that very opposition of subjective and objective upon which it was based. For he mentions that without necessary and universal principles, the experience of things as qualitatively and quantitatively determined objects, coexisting in space and passing through changes in time (or even the determination of the successive states of the subject as successive), would itself have been impossible. Hence necessity of thought cannot be derived from a frequent experience of such objects. It is true that the determination of things as permanent substances, reciprocally acting on each other according to universal laws, goes beyond the determination of them as qualified and quantified phenomena in space and time. But both determinations are possible only through the same *a priori* principle, and we cannot admit the former determination without implicitly admitting the latter. As, therefore, it is through the necessity and universality of thought that objects exist for us, even before the application to them of the principles of scientific induction, and as the application of those principles is only a further step in that *a priori* synthesis which is already involved in the perception of these objects, we have no reason for treating the former kind of synthesis as objectively valid, which does not equally apply to the latter.

This vindication of the principles of induction has, however, a further consequence, which was not clearly seen by Kant. It is fatal to the antithesis of the "given" and the "known," of what is perceived and what is conceived, of *natura materialiter spectata* and *natura formaliter spectata*, which he still admitted. For that antithesis really rested on the idea that there is no universal and necessary principle of determination of things involved in the apprehension of them as qualified and quantified phenomena in space and time. So soon, therefore, as it is seen that there is such a principle, and that the first determination of things as objects of perception is due to the same *a priori* synthesis which in the second place determines them as objects of experience, the ground for that contrast between reality and appearance, on which the theory of induction rested, is taken away. Kant, indeed, finds a new meaning for that contrast by interpreting it as referring, not to the opposition between things as they are given and things as they are known, but to a supposed opposition between things as they are given and known in experience and things as they are in themselves out of experience. This new antithesis of reality and experience, however, only means that the former antithesis has broken down, and that therefore the ideal of knowledge based upon it has yielded to a new ideal. The so-called things in themselves are noumena, the objects of an intuitive or perceptive understanding, *i.e.*, objects in which the contrast of perception and conception, of given and known, is transcended. We can make Kant's theory consistent only by supposing him to mean that the conception of the world as a system of substances determining each other according to universal laws, does not yet satisfy the idea of knowledge which reason brings with it. In other words, just as science, guided by the idea of law or causal connection, found something wanting in the conception of the world as a mere complex of quantified and qualified phenomena in space and time, so philosophy, in view of a still higher ideal of knowledge, may condemn the conception of the world as a system of objects determined by necessary laws of relation, as itself inadequate and imperfect. And we have seen that this higher ideal is that which is involved in the unity of self-consciousness. Unfortunately Kant was unable, as Aristotle had been unable, to distinguish this idea from the idea of an abstract identity in which there is no room for even a relative difference of perception and conception, and therefore the thought of a "perceptive understanding" occurs to him only to be rejected.

If, however, we correct this inadequacy of Kant's statement, as his later works enable us partly to correct it, we see that it involves a new idea of knowledge and a new logic,—a logic governed by the idea of organic unity and development, just as the analytic logic had been governed by the idea of identity, and as the inductive logic had been governed by the idea of necessary law. For, if the unity of self-consciousness be our type of knowledge, truth must mean to us, not the apprehension of objects as self-identical things, distinguished from each other in quantity and quality, nor even the determination of such things as standing in necessary relations to each other. It must mean the determination of the world (and of whatever in the world is in any sense an independent reality, so far as it is so independent) as a unity which realises itself in and through difference, a unity which is indeed determined, but determined by itself. In a view of the world which is governed by this category, correlation must be reinterpreted as organic unity, and causation as development. Its logical method must be neither analytical nor synthetical, or rather it must be both at once, *i.e.*, it must endeavour to exhibit the process of things as the evolution of a unity which is at once self-differentiating and self-integrating, which manifests itself in difference, that through difference it may return upon itself. Further, as this logic arises simply out of a deeper consciousness of that which was contained in the two previous logics, so it first enables us to explain them. In other words, the advance from the analytic to the inductive logic, and again from the inductive to what may be called the genetic logic, may itself be shown to be a self-determined development of thought, in which the first two steps are the imperfect manifestation of a principle fully revealed only in the last step. The consciousness of self-identical objects, independent of each other and of thought, is thus only the beginning of a process of knowledge, which reaches its second stage in the determination of these objects as essentially related to each other, and which finds its ultimate end in the knowledge of the correlated objects as essentially related to the mind that knows them. Or if, in this last point of view, things are still conceived as having a certain relative independence of the mind, it can only be in so far as they are in the Leibnizian sense monads, or microcosms,—*i.e.*, in so far as they are self-determined, and so have, in the narrower circle of their individual life, something analogous to the self-completed nature of the world, when it is contemplated in its unity with its spiritual principle.

Such a genetic logic is inconsistent with any absolute distinction between the *a priori* and *a posteriori* element in knowledge. For here the *a priori* is not simply a law of necessary connection to be applied to an external matter, but a principle of organic development, a principle which, from the very nature of it, cannot be applied to a foreign matter. To treat the world as organic is to apply to it a category which is inconsistent with its being something merely given or externally presented to thought. The relation of things to thought must itself be brought under the same category of organic unity which is applied to the relation of things to each other in the world, otherwise the externality of the world to the thought for which it is, will contradict the conception of the world as itself organic. Hence the distinction of *a priori* and *a posteriori*, so far as it is maintained at all, must shrink to something secondary and relative. It can be maintained only as a distinction of thought from its object, which presupposes their ultimate unity. From this point of view logic may be said to deal with the *a priori*, in so far as it treats the general conditions and methods of knowledge without reference to any particular object. Logic must exhibit abstractly the process by which the intelligence establishes its unity with the intelligible world; or, to put it in another way, it must demonstrate that the being of things can be truly conceived only as their being for thought. It is limited to the *a priori*, in the sense that it ends with the idea that the *esse* of things is their *intelligi*, and does not consider how this real intelligence or intelligible reality manifests itself in the concrete world of nature and spirit.

In this sense logic cannot be separated from metaphysic, if metaphysic be confined to ontology. They are simply two aspects of one science, which we may regard either as determining the idea of being or the idea of knowing. The process of knowing is never really a formal process; it always involves the application of certain categories, and these categories are simply successive definitions of being or reality. We cannot separate the category from the movement of thought by which it is evolved and applied, nor the transition from lower to higher categories from changes of logical method. Hence a logic divorced from metaphysic inevitably becomes empty and unreal, and a metaphysic divorced from logic reduces itself to a kind of dictionary of abstract terms, which are put in no living relation to each other. For such a logic and such a metaphysic must rest on the assumption of an absolute division between being and thought, the very two terms the unity of which it must be the utmost object of both logic and metaphysic to prove and to produce.

4. *The Relation of Metaphysic to Philosophy of Religion.*—The possibility of a "first philosophy," as we have already seen, is essentially bound up

with the possibility of what we may call a "last philosophy." It is only in so far as we can rise above the point of view of the individual and the dualism of the ordinary consciousness,—in so far, in other words, as we can have at least an anticipative consciousness of that *last* unity, in which all the differences of things from each other and from the mind that knows them are explained and transcended,—that we are able to go back to that *first* unity which all these differences presuppose. The life of man begins with a divided consciousness, with a consciousness of self which is opposed to the consciousness of what is not-self, with a consciousness of a multiplicity of particulars which do not seem to be bound together by any one universal principle. Such division and apparent independence of what are really parts of one whole is characteristic of nature, and in spirit it is at first only so far transcended that it has become conscious of itself. A conscious difference, however, as it is a difference in consciousness, is no longer an unmediated difference. It is a difference through which the unity has begun to show itself, and which therefore that unity is on the way to subordinate. And all the development of consciousness and self-consciousness is just the process through which this subordination is carried out, up to the point at which the difference is seen to be nothing but the manifestation of the unity. Just so far, therefore, as this end is present to us,—so far as we are able to look forward to the solution or reconciliation of all the divisions and oppositions of which we are conscious, and to see that there is an all-embracing unity which they cannot destroy,—is it possible that we should look back to the beginning or first unity, and recognise that these divisions and oppositions are but the manifestations of it. Thus the extremes of abstractness and of concreteness of thought are bound up together. The freedom of intelligence which enables us to free ourselves from the complexity of our actual life, and to direct our thoughts to the simplest and most elementary conditions of being and knowing, is possible only to those who are not limited to that life, but can regard it and all its finite concerns from the point of view of the infinite and the universal. In this sense it is true that religion and metaphysic spring from the same source, and that it is possible to vindicate the rationality of religion only on metaphysical principles. The philosophy of religion is, in fact, only the last application or final expression of metaphysic; and, conversely, a metaphysic which is not capable of furnishing an explanation of religion, contradicts itself.

This last remark affords us a kind of criterion of a true metaphysic. Can it or can it not explain religion? If it cannot, it must be equally unable to explain its own possibility, and therefore implicitly it condemns itself. Thus a pantheistic system, which loses the subject in the Absolute, cannot explain how that subject should apprehend the substance of which it is but a transitory mode, nor, on the other hand, can it explain why the substance should manifest itself in and to a subject. And the same criticism may be made on all theories in which the first or metaphysical unity is abstractly opposed to the manifoldness and contingency of things. Not only of Spinoza, but also of Kant, of Fichte, and even of Schelling, it might with some truth be said that their absolute is like the lion's den in the fable; for all the footsteps are directed towards it, and none seem to issue from it. It is essential that the first unity should be such as to explain the possibility of difference and division; for, if it is not, then the return to unity out of difference is made as accidental as the difference itself. Thus when Aristotle represented the Divine Being as pure self-consciousness, pure .form without matter, he found himself unable to account for the existence of any world in which form was realised in matter. When therefore he speaks of the process of the finite world by which it returns to God, and attributes to nature a will, which is directed to the good as its final cause, his theory seems to be little more than a metaphor in which the analogy of consciousness is applied to the unconscious. For, if the Divine Being is not manifested in the world, any tendency of the world to realise the good becomes an inexplicable fact. A similar difficulty is, as we saw, involved in Kant's confusion of the bare identity of understanding with the absolute unity of knowledge. Reducing the unity of self-consciousness to such a bare identity, Kant could not be expected to see, what Aristotle had not seen, that pure self-consciousness is essentially related to anything but itself. Hence the various attempts which he made, in his ethical works and in his *Critique of Judgment*, to find a link of connection between the noumenal and the empirical, were necessarily condemned even by himself as the expressions of a merely regulative or subjective principle of knowledge. Even Fichte, who found in the idea of self-consciousness a principle of differentiation and integration—which explained how self-consciousness in us should be necessarily correlative with the consciousness of a world—was, at least in his earlier and more important works, unable to free himself from the Kantian opposition of a noumenal identity which is without difference to a phenomenal unity which is realised in difference. Hence by him also the return out of difference is regarded as an impossibility, or as a *processus in infinitum*, and the absolute unity as that which is beyond all knowledge and only apprehended by faith.

If we look to completely elaborated theories, and disregard all tentative and imperfect sketches, it may fairly be said that all that has as yet been done in the region of pure metaphysic is summed up in two works, in the *Metaphysic* of Aristotle and the *Logic* of Hegel. And, up to a certain point, the lesson which they teach is one and the same, viz., that the ultimate unity which is presupposed in all differences is the unity of thought with itself, the unity of self-consciousness, and that in this unity is contained the type of all science, and the form of all existence; in other words, that $I = I$ is the formula of the universe. The difference between these two works has, however, already been indicated. With Aristotle, in so far as he neglects the essential relation of self-consciousness to consciousness, or of the conscious self to the world of objects in space and time, the unity of self-consciousness tends to pass, as it did pass with the Neo-Platonists, into a pure identity without difference. In the Hegelian logic, on the other hand, self-consciousness is interpreted as a unity which realises itself through difference and the reconciliation of difference,—as, in fact, an organic unity of elements, which exist only as they pass into each other. In other words, it is shown that the differentiating movement, by which the subjective and the objective self are opposed, and the integrating movement, by which they are reunited, are both essential. Hence we cannot think of the conscious self as a simple resting identity, but only as an active self-determining principle; nor can we think of its self-determination as a pure affirmation of itself without any negation, but only as an affirmation which involves a double negation—an opposition of two elements which yet are essentially united. Each factor in this unity, in fact, is necessarily conceived as passing beyond itself into the other; the subject is subject, only as it relates itself to the object, the object is object, only as it relates itself to the subject. It is this tension against each other of elements which yet are correlated and indissolubly united, this self-surrender to each other of elements which yet are maintained in their distinction, that constitutes the organic unity of thought in itself, and separates it from the mere abstract unity of mysticism.

When, however, the concrete or self-differentiating character of the unity of self-consciousness is apprehended in this way,—so that it is impossible to confuse its indivisible unity with the simplicity of that which is one with itself merely because it has no differences in it,—the problem of the relation of pure self-consciousness to the world in space and time ceases to be insoluble. Thought, as it is seen to have difference in itself, is no longer irreconcilable with the world of difference; nor is it necessary to introduce a foreign ὕλη to make their connection intelligible. For, as thought is a principle of difference as well as of unity, of analysis as well as of synthesis, and as it cannot realise itself in its unity except through the utmost development of difference, abstract self-consciousness, with its transparent or merely ideal difference, cannot be its ultimate form. On the contrary, the consciousness of self is possible only in distinction from, and in relation to, a world of objects. In other words, the unity of the thinking subject presupposes, not merely the opposition of the subjective and the objective self, but also the opposition of the self in its pure self-identity to a world of externality and difference. The pure intelligence, which is the *prius* of all things, must not, therefore, be regarded—as Aristotle regarded it—as merely theoretical, but also as practical. It must be conceived as a living principle, a principle which only in self-manifestation can be conscious of itself, and to the very nature of which, therefore, self-manifestation is essential. In this way Hegel—just because he grasped the concrete character of the unity of thought in itself—was enabled to understand the necessary unity of thought or self-consciousness with the world, and to heal the division of physics from metaphysic, which Aristotle had left unexplained.

Schelling and others who have raised objections to the Hegelian method have specially directed their criticisms against this transition from logic to the philosophy of nature, from pure self-consciousness to the external world in space and time. In doing so, they have practically fallen back upon the Aristotelian theory, with its opposition of God, as pure form, to the finite world. But this in effect is to deny that "the real is the rational or intelligible," and to introduce into the world, as the ground of its distinction from reason, a purely irrational or contingent element. A modern disciple of Schelling's later positive philosophy [1] only draws the necessary consequence from this view, when he teaches the pessimist creed that the highest good is the negation or extinction of the finite. Nor can we wonder that the same writer, who denies that the absolute self-consciousness is essentially related to or manifested in the world, should proceed to reduce

[1] Von Hartmann.

this self-consciousness to a mystic identity, which comes out of itself and becomes self-conscious only by an inscrutable act of will. The fact, indeed, that those who deny the possibility of a rational transition from self-consciousness to the world, are forced by the logic of their position to reduce self-consciousness to an abstract identity, may be regarded as a kind of indirect proof that the principle of self-consciousness, truly conceived, does involve that transition.

Another step in the same direction may be made if we consider how the Cartesian philosophy treated the opposition between subject and object, which it also regarded as absolute. By Des Cartes mind and matter, thought and extension, are defined as abstract opposites, every quality of each finding its contradictory counterpart in a quality of the other. Mind is a pure self-determined unity, which is as it knows itself and knows itself as it is, which has no discretion of parts or capacity of division or determination from without. Matter is essentially discrete or infinitely divided; it is a pure passivity; and all its determination comes to it from without. The world is therefore, as it were, "cut in two with a hatchet," divided into two unrelated existences, which are held together only by the will of God. Spinoza cuts the knot, and avoids the arbitrariness of this solution, by treating extension and thought as two attributes, separated in relation to our intelligence, but each expressing fully the absolute substance. And something like the same view has been revived in recent times, by writers like Lewes and Mr. Spencer, who speak of feelings and motions as two opposite "aspects" of the same fact. When we ask, however, *for whom* these attributes or aspects are a unity, it becomes clear that the intelligence, which is regarded as standing on one side of the dualism, must also be taken as transcending it, and relating the two sides to each other. Moreover, the correspondence of the two attributes upon which Spinoza insists, and their contrariety upon which Des Cartes insists, when taken together, give us the idea of a correlative opposition, *i.e.*, of an opposition of elements which yet are necessary to each other. If, therefore, they cannot be simply identified as Spinoza identifies them, yet they need no external bond such as Des Cartes introduces to combine them; for they cannot exist apart from each other.

Their opposition is held within the limits of their unity, and is no absolute contradiction, but rather an opposition which exists only as it is transcended. In other words, it is an abstract opposition, *i.e.*, it is an opposition of elements which seem to be irreconcilable, till it is observed that they are correlative, that each exists or has a meaning only as it relates itself to, or passes out of itself into, the other, and that each, held in its abstraction and separation from the other, loses all the meaning that it seemed to have. For, as in an organic body each member or organ lives only in tension against the others, yet only as continually relating itself to the others, so the utmost opposition of mind to matter, of the intelligence to the intelligible world, presupposes their unity, and is only the realisation of it.

There is here, however, something more than an ordinary case of correlation, for in this unity of opposites *mind* appears twice—once as one of the opposites, and again as the unity which transcends the opposition. This ambiguity becomes most obvious in theories like that of Mr. Spencer, who speaks of "two consciousnesses," which cannot be resolved into each other, but yet which strangely form inseparable parts of one and the same consciousness. What, however, is really involved in such a statement is that the external world, which in the first instance presents itself as absolutely opposed to the subject whose object it is, is yet one with that subject, and that therefore the antagonism of mind to its object is only the last differentiation through which it realises its unity with itself. In Hegel's language, that which presents itself as other than mind is *its* other—" an other which is not another," whose difference and opposition to itself it overreaches and overcomes. We must, therefore, regard the independence and externality of nature, its indifference, and even, as it seems, opposition, to the development of the moral and intellectual life of man, as merely apparent. For man, in this point of view, is not merely one natural being among others, but *the* being in whom nature is at once completed and transcended. If, therefore, at first he appears to stand in merely accidental and external relations to the other existences among which he finds himself, yet the whole process of his life,—the process by which he comes to know the external world, and by which, reacting upon it, he makes it the means to the realisation of an individual and social life of his own,—is the negation of this contingency and externality. In all this process he is showing himself to be a being who can know himself only as he knows the objective world, and who can realise himself only as he makes himself the agent of a divine purpose, to which all things are contributing.

Such an idea of man's relation to the world is necessarily involved in any theory that goes beyond that subjective idealism or sensationalism, which denies to him every object of knowledge except his own states of feeling, and every end of action except his own pleasures and pains. Recent speculation, indeed, has suggested a compromise by which this dilemma is supposed to be evaded, and mankind are represented as forming an organic unity in themselves, though they are still conceived as standing in an external and accidental relation to nature, the forces of which by their knowledge and skill they have subdued and are more and more subduing to their service. Such a compromise we find in the philosophy of Comte, the first writer who, starting from an apparently empirical basis, was able to break through the individualistic prejudices of the school of Locke. In the latter volumes of his *Positive Philosophy*, still more in his *Positive Politics*, Comte so far transcends individualism as to deny the externality of men to each other, and to declare that "the individual, as such, is an abstraction," and that in reality he cannot be separated from the social organism, which is thus not merely an extraneous condition of his development, but essential to his very existence as man. Thus individual men exist only through the universal—through the spirit of the family, of the nation, of humanity, which manifests itself in them as a principle of life and development. Yet this organic unity, according to Comte, is in contact with a world, which in relation to it is external and contingent. Nature has not its final cause in man, but on the contrary is, at first, rather his enemy; and it is to humanity itself that the praise is due if to a certain extent the enemy has been turned into a servant. The unity of life which manifests itself in humanity cannot therefore be considered as a universal principle, as the principle of the whole universe, but simply as the principle of the limited existence of man, which is hemmed in on every side by external and, in the main, unknown conditions. If humanity therefore is an organism, it is an organism existing in a medium which, in reference to it, is inorganic, *i.e.*, in a medium which has no essential relation to the life that animates man.

It is obvious, however, that this theory is an illogical attempt to find a standing ground between two opposite philosophies,—between the philosophy which treats man merely as a natural individual, placed among other individual beings and things, and which therefore regards his relation to them as something accidental and external and the philosophy which treats him as a spiritual subject, a conscious and self-conscious being, and regards him therefore as having no *merely* external relations either to other men or to nature. Comte shrinks from regarding the world without us as the manifestation of that spiritual principle which is also within us, which constitutes our very nature as individual men, and which therefore connects us with the world at the same time that it separates us from it. Yet he recognises the existence in us of a principle which is so far universal that it constitutes a community between all men. He thinks that the individual can transcend himself, so far as to see all things, not indeed from a divine point of view, *sub specie æternitatis*, but from the point of view of universal humanity, and that in conformity with this theoretical consciousness, he can live a practical life of altruism, *i.e.*, a life in which he identifies his own good with the good of humanity. But the philosophy that has gone so far, must logically go further. It is impossible to treat humanity as an organism without extending the organic idea to the conditions under which the social life of humanity is developed. The medium by aid of which, or in reacting against which, the organised being maintains itself, is an essential part of its life; it remains organic, only in so far as it can mould itself to its conditions and its conditions to itself. This is true even of the animal organism in relation to the small circle of its environment, which, however, is part of a larger circle of conditions to which the animal has no relation. But a conscious being is a *universal* centre of relations; there is nothing which he, as conscious, cannot make part of his own life. Hence the application of the organic idea to him involves its application to the whole world. And, if the recognition of a universal principle manifested in humanity naturally led Comte to the idea of the worship of humanity, the recognition of a universal principle manifested in man and nature alike must lead to the idea of the worship of God.[1]

The rationality of religion, then, rests on the possibility of an ultimate synthesis, in which man and nature are regarded as the manifestation of one spiritual principle. For religion involves a faith that, in our efforts to realise the good of humanity, we are not merely straining after an ideal beyond us, which may or may not be realised, but are animated by a principle which, within us and without us, is necessarily realising itself, because it is the ultimate principle by which all things are, and are known. This absolute certitude of religion, that man can work effectually because all the universe is working with him, or, in other words, because God is working in him, can find its explanation and defence only in a philosophy for which ".the real is the rational, and the rational is the real." And such a philosophy, beginning with the Kantian doctrine that existence means existence for a spiritual or thinking subject, must go on to

[1] This criticism of Comte is more fully developed in my book on *The Social Philosophy and Religion of Comte*.

prove that *that* only can exist for such a subject, which is the manifestation of thought or spirit; and conversely, that spirit or intelligence is essentially self-manifesting, or, in other words, that it cannot be conceived except as standing in essential relation to an external and material world. Finally, if nature be thus regarded as a necessary manifestation of spirit, it can be opposed to spirit only in so far as spirit in its realisation becomes opposed to itself. In other words, nature must be regarded as, from a higher point of view, included in spirit. Nature exists that it may show itself to be spiritual in and to man, who transcends it yet implies it, who finds in it the necessary basis of his thought and action, but only that he may build upon it a higher spiritual life.

> "Nature is made better by no mean
> But nature makes that mean: so over the art
> Which, you say, adds to nature is an art
> Which nature makes."

Only the order of precedence suggested by these words must be inverted. For, as nature is only *for* spirit, so the spiritual energy which reacts upon nature is that which manifests for the first time what nature in reality is. It is the consciousness of this, *i.e.*, of the identity of that which is realising itself within and without us,—the consciousness that the necessity which is the precondition of our freedom is the manifestation of the very principle which makes us free—that turns morality into religion. For it is this alone which enables us to regard the realisation of the highest ends of human life neither as a happy accident, nor as a conquest to be won by the cunning of man from an unfriendly or indifferent destiny, but as the result towards which all things are working.

In this philosophy, which finds its most adequate expression in the works of Hegel, there are two things which may be distinguished—the general idealistic view of the world, and the dialectical movement of thought in which Hegel develops and expresses it. And there are perhaps many at the present time who are prepared to accept the former, but who yet suspect, or even reject, the latter. And no doubt there is much in Hegel's *Logic* and *Philosophy of Spirit*, and still more in his *Philosophy of Nature*, which there is reason to regard with distrust. In clever hands that are not checked by a sufficient consciousness of the whole, the

Hegelian dialectic may be made into the means of producing a seeming proof of anything. Nor is it always easy to determine how far Hegel himself was tempted, by an impatient consciousness of the universality of his method, to employ it in cases where the conditions of its successful application were wanting. Sometimes he seems to forget, what he himself teaches, that science must first have generalised experience and determined it by its finite categories, ere it is possible for philosophy to give its final interpretation. Yet, when we realise the nature of that interpretation, and of the transformation of science which philosophy by means of it proposes to effect, it becomes clear that the dialectic of Hegel is no extraneous addition to his idealism, but is part and parcel of the same movement of thought. For that dialectic rests on the idea that thought or self-consciousness finds in its own organic unity the ultimate key to all difficulties in regard to the objects of thought, as well as in regard to their relations to each other and to the mind. Self-consciousness, as has been already shown, is itself implicitly the whole web of categories, which it throws over the world, and by aid of which it makes the world intelligible. All these it contains in itself; and, as it proceeds to determine the meaning of things, it simply produces its store, and exhausts itself on the object. Now, if it be essential to idealism, to make thought or self-consciousness the principle and ultimate explanation of all that exists, it is obvious that we cannot separate idealism from some such dialectic as this,—a dialectic which is nothing more than the mind's consciousness of its own movement or process of self-affirmation. If to find thought in things be more than an empty word, then the movement or process, which thought *is*, must explain at once the transition from thought to what in opposition we call "things," and must give us the means of reconciling that opposition. In other words, the same movement by which thought determines itself as self-conscious, *i.e.*, as a unity realised through difference, must also be conceived as the explanation of the difference *between* pure thought and the world, and as the solution of that difference in the idea of absolute spirit.

Such idealism has a close relation to Christianity; it may be even said to be but Christianity theorised. It has often been asserted that Hegel's philosophy of religion is but an artificial accommodation to Christian doctrine of a philosophy which has no inherent relation to Christianity. If, however, we regard the actual development of Hegel's thought, it would be truer to say that it was the study of Christian ideas which first produced the Hegelian philosophy. What delivered Hegel from the mysticism in which the later philosophies of Fichte and Schelling tended to lose themselves, and led him, in his own language, to regard the absolute "not merely as substance but as subject,"—what made him recognise with Fichte that the absolute principle is spiritual, and yet enabled him with Schelling to see in nature, as the opposite of spirit, the very means of its realisation,—was his thorough appreciation of the ethical and religious meaning of Christianity. In the great Christian aphorism that "he .who loseth his life alone can save it" he found a key to the difficulties of ethics, a reconciliation of hedonism and asceticism. For what this saying implies is that a spiritual or self-conscious being is one who is in contradiction with himself, when he makes his individual self his end. In opposing his own interest to that of others, he is preventing their interests from becoming his; all things are his, and his only, who has died to himself. But if this be the truth of morality, it is something more, for "morality is the nature of things." We cannot separate the law of the life of man from the law of the world in which he lives. And, if it is the nature of things, as it is the nature of spirit, that he who loseth his life shall save it, the world must be referred to a spiritual principle, and the Christian doctrine of the nature of God is only the converse of the Christian law of ethics. To Hegel, starting from this point, a new light was thrown on the Fichtean treatment of the idea of self, and the Fichtean proof that the consciousness of self implies a relation to an object, an object which is opposed to the self, and which yet from another point of view—since an object exists only for a subject—cannot be anything but an element of its own life. It was seen that this movement of thought is no mere fluctuation between contradictory positions, to be terminated finally by an *ipse dixit* of faith, but that the unity of the opposite elements is apprehensible by the intelligence, and that indeed it is *its* presence to the intelligence which makes the consciousness of opposition possible. It was in this sense that

Hegel could say that that unity of opposites, which had been called unintelligible by previous writers, was just the very nature of the intelligence,[1] and that only a view of the world guided by this idea could be properly intelligible, while every other view must contain in it an unsolved contradiction, an element that remains permanently impervious to thought.

The great objection to a metaphysic like this, at least an objection which weighs much in the minds of many, is that which springs from the contrast between the claim of absolute knowledge, which it seems to involve, and the actual limitations which our intelligence encounters in every direction. If the theory were true—it is felt, or thought—we ought to be nearer the solution of the problems of our life, practical and speculative, than we are; the riddle of the painful earth ought to vex us less; we ought to be able to find our way more easily through the entanglement of facts, and to deal with practical difficulties in a less tentative manner. Yet there is really no antagonism between such a doctrine and a consciousness of the limitation of our faculties; nay rather, it is only on such a

[1] *Logik*, iii. p. 256, seq.

theory that a rational distrust of ourselves can be based. When Aristotle meets the warning that we should think finite and human things, since we are finite and human, with the answer that we ought rather, so far as in us lies, to rise to what is immortal and divine, he is not denying the limits of man's knowledge and power; on the contrary, he is rather pointing to the very principle which makes us conscious of those limits. For it is just because there is in man a principle of infinity that he knows his finitude, and, conversely, it is just in the *consciousness* of this finitude that he rises above it. A rational humility is possible only to one who has in himself the measure of his own weakness, and who, if he "trembles like a guilty thing surprised," is yet conscious that he is trembling before himself. This truth is often expressed by Kant with special relation to the moral consciousness, as where he contrasts the limitation of man, as a sensible being occupying an infinitesimal space in the boundless world of sense, with his freedom from all limitation as a personal self, a member of the truly infinite world of intelligence. But it is not necessary to adopt Kant's abstract division of the sensible from the intelligible world, to see that our consciousness of the greatness of the problem to be solved in human life and thought, is deepened and widened by that very idea of philosophy, which yet gives us the assurance that the problem is not insoluble, and even that, in principle, it is already solved.

INDEX.

Absolute, An, Comte's attitude towards, 199.
— Possibility of a philosophy without, 200.
— Consciousness of, 225, 515.
Abstraction, its philosophic defect, 293, 341, 394, 395, 396.
Agnosticism, 206.
— Modern, 220, 224.
— Ancient, 220.
Altruism, 529.
Ambulo ergo sum, 273.
Analytic, 409, 410, 415, 428.
Analytic, Prior, 493.
Analytic, Posterior, 456, 493, 496, 503.
Antinomies, 434.
Antithesis. See *Opposition*.
Aristotle, 384, 418, 485, 503, 538,
— and problem of philosophy, 211.
— criticism of Plato, 367, 396-7, 455, 458.
— on metaphysic, 385-9, 391, 473, 485-6, 493.
— view of knowledge, 456-9, 495-7.
— on relation of intelligence to intelligible world, 468, 484-6, 521.
— as analytic philosopher, 481-2.
— on *tabula rasa*, 489.
— view of logic, 492, 497.
— on pure identity, 508, 518.
— on pure intelligence, 516, 520, 521.
Arnauld, 322.
Arnold, Matthew, 147, 153.

Art, its function, 61, 62.
Asceticism, Early, 22.
— in middle ages, 22, 23.
— an element in Christianity, 96, 99.
— Spinoza's attitude towards, 378.
Awakening of Epimenides, 67.

Bacon, 195, 269, 338, 399, 462, 483, 504.
Being, Thought and, 274-6, 286-7, 404, 447.
— Science of, 385-9.
— Notion of, 385, 393, 431.
— Knowing and, 412.
Bentham, 378.
Bible and Protestantism, 135.
Biography, 238.
Blyenbergh, 355.
Bonagiunto di Lucca, 6.
Boniface VIII., 41.
Bossuet, 137.
Burke, Edmund, 120.
Byron, 78, 169.

Cacciaguida, 33.
Calvin, 134.
Campaign in France, 91.
Can Grande della Scala, 9, 30, 39.
Carlyle, admiration of Goethe, 10, 84, 232.
— Influence of, on modern thought, 231, 236.
— German literature and, 233, 245, 248.

Carlyle, his relation to political and social life, 234, 261 *sqq.*
— Froude's biography of, 238.
— Attitude of present generation towards, 240.
— Historical works of, 241, 258, 261.
— literary characteristics, 241, 245, 246, 248, 260.
— attitude towards metaphysics, 248, 250.
— his humour and imagination, 250, 258.
— his paradoxes, 251, 255, 259, 260.
— place given by him to work, 252.
— — to faith, 252.
— hero-worship, 262.
— his individualism, 264.
Cartesianism, 267-382.
— relation to modern spirit, 268, 382.
— aim, 269.
— method, 270.
— underlying principle, 278.
— Inconsistencies in, 291, 292, 305.
— Characteristics of, 293, 382, 465.
— Dualism of, 306, 310, 352, 358, 362, 368, 522.
— Development of, by Malebranche, 268, 310-332; by Spinoza, 268, 332-381.
— See also *Des Cartes, Malebranche, Spinoza.*
Causality, Law of, 287, 402, 418, 421, 449, 476, 484, 504, 509.
Celestine, Pope, 41.
Chance, Aristotle's idea of, 459.
Characteristics, 249.
Characteristics of the Present Age, Fichte's, 250.
Chartism, 243, 261.
Chasdai Creskas, 232.
Christianity, Characteristics of, in Apostolic Ages, 13, 17, 20, 215.
— — in Early Church, 17, 19, 22.
— — in Middle Ages, 10, 21, 25, 35 *sqq.*, 397, 460, 488.
— Inherent Characteristics of, 16,

45, 47, 49, 96, 99, 216, 225, 361, 396, 535.
Christianity, Goethe's attitude towards, 85, 96 *sqq.*
— — Rousseau's, 138.
— — Carlyle's, 256.
— — Hegel's, 534-6.
Church, Catholic, 135, 137, 144, 460.
— See also *Christianity.*
Cogito ergo sum, 272, 274, 278, 284.
Comte, 218, 488.
— his view of man and the world, 197 *sqq.*, 526 *sqq.*
Confessions, The, 107, 111, 117, 186.
Consciousness of the infinite, 192-3, 207-8, 221, 224-5, 269, 278 *sqq.*, 318 *sqq.*, 464, 477.
— of the finite, 192-3, 207-8, 221, 224, 281 *sqq.*, 290, 317, 475-7.
— of the external world, 192-3, 201, 222, 269, 270, 274-8, 316, 318, 394, 398, 408, 413 *sqq.*, 433 *sqq.*, 447-8, 470-7, 486, 500, 517 *sqq.*
— See also *Experience.*
— of self, 192-3, 201, 222, 269, 272 *sqq.*, 283-7, 290, 316 *sqq.*, 404, 413, 426 *sqq.*, 471, 513 *sqq.*, 536.
— See also *Self-consciousness.*
— Process of, 269, 270, 403, 429, 451, 457, 472-8, 490, 513, 514.
— Unity of, 404, 428 *sqq.*, 469.
— Empirical, 417, 424, 428, 441.
— Moral, 417, 421, 538.
Conscious being or subject, 403, 447, 470-7, 489, 529.
Contradiction, Law of, 387, 465, 485, 495, 497-8.
Contrat Social, 121, 123, 124.
Credo ut intelligam, 460, 461.
Critical Philosophy of Kant, 411.
Critique of Judgment, 70, 71, 419, 420, 516.
Critique of Practical Reason, 417, 419.
Critique of Pure Reason, 205, 404, 406, 407, 416, 419.

Dante, Controversy on opinions of, 1.
— characteristics as a poet, 5 *sqq.*, 11, 46, 47.
— Dualism of, 24, 29, 34, 45.
— relation to mediæval Catholicism, 3, 10, 35 *sqq.*
— — to philosophy, 5, 6, 8, 38, 48, 50.
— — to the Roman Empire, 35, 42.
— transcends the mediæval Dualism, 34, 49, 51.
Darwin, 467, 471.
Deism, 141.
De Anima, 387, 457, 468, 494.
De Deo et Homini, 333, 368.
De Emendatione Intellectus, 338, 344, 349.
De Monarchia, 35, 36, 37, 44.
De omnibus dubitandum est, 270.
Des Cartes, 267-310, 332, 465.
— founder of modern philosophy, 268.
— his aim, 269, 287.
— his method, 270 *sqq.*, 278.
— his first principle, 272 *sqq.*, 283, 376.
— his conception of God, 278 *sqq.*, 285-9, 292-7, 301, 306, 313, 361.
— — of relation between finite and infinite, 282 *sqq.*, 292 *sqq.*, 352.
— his dualism, 276, 287-8, 294, 300, 304, 310, 315, 368, 522-3.
— relation to pantheism, 284.
— his theories of error, 289.
— — of freedom of the will, 294, 324, 372.
— — of knowledge, 296, 465.
— — of innate ideas, 296.
— — of truth, 297.
— — of external world, 297, 301, 318.
— — of matter and mind, 300 *sqq.*, 434, 522-3.
— — of animal life, 302.
— — of union of body and soul, 304.
— — of the passions, 307-8.
Desires, 427.

Descriptive Sketches, 164, 166.
Determination, Self-, 469, 476.
— from without, 469, 476,
Development, Goethe and idea of, 86, 91, 94, 104.
— and human spirit, 209, 466, 468, 470.
— Darwin's theory of, 467, 471.
Dialectic, Aristotle's, 405, 409, 411, 428, 429.
Dichtung und Wahrheit, 76, 80.
Discourse on the Causes of Inequality, 120, 123.
Divina Commedia, 5.
— its theme, 9.
— its dualism, 10, 29, 34, 38.
— its place in Middle Ages, 52.
— Purgatorio, 6, 7, 30, 32, 33, 39, 46.
— Paradiso, 8, 9, 30, 33, 35, 41, 51, 52.
— Inferno, 30, 31, 32, 35, 40, 46, 52.
Dualism in Middle Ages, 12, 22, 25, 28, 35, 396.
— in Early Church, 13, 396.
— in Greek philosophy, 227, 396, 454, 458, 496.
— in Scholastic philosophy, 397, 460, 482-3, 488.
— in Modern philosophy, 276, 287-8, 292 *sqq.*, 315, 330, 352 *sqq.*, 376, 398 *sqq.*, 480 *sqq.*, 523.
— See also *Opposition*.

Education, Rousseau's plan of, 122, 125, 128.
— Wordsworth's treatment of, 183.
Emile, 122, 125, 127, 128.
Empire, Roman, 14, 35, 36, 38, 42.
Encyclopædists, 161.
English Lake District as interpreted in the Poems of Wordsworth, 150.
Entia rationis, 349, 353, 356.
Entretien, 316, 327.
Epicureans, 200, 221.
Epinay, Mémoires de Madame d', 114.

INDEX.

Epistle to the Bishop of Llandaff, 162, 166.
Epistolæ, 297, 303, 354, 357, 359, 363, 369, 380.
Erasmus, 269.
Erdmann, 363.
Error, 289, 328, 485.
Essay on Winckelmann, 88.
Essay on Human Understanding, 443.
Ethics, The, 69, 70, 333, 334, 340, 345, 346, 349, 350, 359, 364, 370, 371, 373, 374, 377, 378, 379, 380, 381, 401.
Excursion, The, 164.
Experience, relation to metaphysic, 387, 389-392, 396, 399-416, 426 *sqq.*, 456-8, 484 *sqq.*
— Ordinary view of, 407.
— Kant's view of, 408 *sqq.*, 420-4, 437, 442, 503-4.
— Objects of, 407-412, 416, 424, 445, 506.
— Form of, 409.
— Inner, 201, 400-2, 405, 463.
— Outer, 201, 399, 400-1, 405, 463.

Faust, 88, 95, 210.
Fichte, 71, 233, 245, 248, 435, 436, 437, 535, 536.
France, in the 18th century, 73-117.
— Wordsworth's attitude towards, 162, 164, 166.
French Revolution, The, 241, 261.
Freedom, Idea of, 418-9, 422, 468.
— and necessity, 421, 451, 532.
Friars, Mendicant, 40.
Froude, J. A., 238, 263.

Gassendi, 273.
Geulincx, 306.
God, Conceptions of, 99, 134, 137, 225, 287, 464.
— — The Mediæval, 49.
— — Goethe's, 85.
— — Rousseau's, 131, 141, 173.
— — Wordsworth's, 173.

God, Conceptions of, Des Cartes', 278 *sqq.*, 285-9, 292-7, 301, 306, 313, 361, 522.
— — Malebranche's, 311 *sqq.*
— — Spinoza's, 350, 357 *sqq.*, 370.
— — Aristotle's, 388-9, 396, 516.
— — Kant's, 416, 420.
— a term of thought, 200, 206, 350.
— Ontological argument for, 287.
Goethe, 54, 155, 170, 210, 232, 235.
— attitude towards philosophy, 65, 68, 72.
— attitude towards Nature, 68, 75.
— attitude towards theology and Christianity, 74, 85, 96.
— — towards philosophers—
  Spinoza, 69, 72, 80.
  Kant, 70.
  Fichte, 71.
  Schelling, 71.
  Voltaire, 73.
  Rousseau, 75, 80.
— self-limitation, 66.
— relation to the past, 72, 88.
— storm and stress period, 75, 84.
— idea of renunciation, 80.
— practical philosophy, 83.
— Hellenic period, 84, 87, 93, 97, 100.
— scientific views, 90, 104.
— limitations of his genius, 95.
— his task, 104.
Goody Blake and Harry Gill, 181.
Götter Griechenlands, 89.
Götz von Berlichingen, 88.
Greece, Goethe and, 87, 93, 100.
— its religion, 87, 212, 215.
— its morality, 212.

Hamilton, Sir William, 444.
Hegel, 332.
— and religion, 18, 215, 479, 534 *sqq.*
— relation to Kant, 430, 436 *sqq.*
— his method, 521 *sqq.*
— philosophy of nature, 525 *sqq.*
Heraclites, 495-6.
Herder, 70.

Heroes and Hero-worship, 264.
Hettinger, 3.
History, Carlyle's treatment of, 241, 257, 258, 261.
Hobbes, 275.
Homer, 10, 56, 155.
Humanity, Conceptions of, Rousseau's, 119, 178, 185.
— — Wordsworth's, 179, 185.
— — Comte's, 199, 204, 526, 530.
— — Herbert Spencer's, 403.
— — Kant's, 406, 418, 420.
— — in Greek religion, 215.
— See also *Man*.
Hume, 504.
Hutton, 184.
Huxley, Professor, 193, 422.

Idealism, Later German, 71, 245, 256, 408, 430 *sqq.*, 469, 498 *sqq.*
— Cartesian, 277, 362.
Ideas, Innate, 296, 465.
— Association of, 504,
Identity, of the self, 409, 413, 426.
— of thought, 410, 424, 432.
— of knowing and being, 412.
— Pure, 423, 426, 427, 435, 445, 508, 518, 522.
— of formal logic, 428, 431, 497-8.
— Aristotle's conception of, 485-6, 494.
Idiot Boy, The, 181.
Idola, 462, 490.
Index, The, 3.
Individual, The, as related to the external world, 469-528.
— as related to the universal, 473, 478-9, 528.
Individualism, Rousseau's, 123, 128, 134, 146, 172, 185.
— Protestant, 134, 382.
— Wordsworth's, 185-6.
— Greek, 220-1.
— Carlyle's, 264.
— of 18th century, 383.
— Comte and, 527.
Induction, Necessity of, 456-7, 504-6.

Induction, Process of, 493.
Infinite. See *Consciousness*.
Italienische Reise, 103.

Jacobi, 68, 98.
Jacobins, The, 116.
Jacopone di Todi, 41, 47.
Judgments, Particular, 451-2.

Kant and immortality, 27.
— on imagination, 60, 251.
— and Goethe, 70.
— on philosophic synthesis, 205,
— on experience and thought, 208.
— on the self, 272.
— on relation of finite to infinite, 281.
— criticism of Des Cartes, 288.
— on relation to Cartesianism, 383, 465.
— on relativity between thought and being, 383, 404 *sqq.*, 440-2.
— on knowledge, 404 *sqq.*, 412-5, 423-4, 431-3, 445.
— his dualism, 405, 407, 409-12, 416, 419-23, 431 *sqq.*
— definition of reason, 412.
— definition of *noumena*, 415.
— on unity of reason and unity of experience, 412.
— his dualism not absolute, 417 *sqq.*, 425, 434, 445, 465-6, 469.
— on self-consciousness, 428-30, 433-6.
— on function of metaphysic, 438.
— Logic of, 508.
Kingdom of ends, 420.
Knowledge, Theories of,
— — Comte's, 197.
— — Des Cartes', 296, 465.
— — Malebranche's, 311 *sqq.*
— — Spinoza's, 340 *sqq.*, 401.
— — Leibniz, 465, 467.
— — Locke's, 465.
— — Socratic, 451-2.
— — Plato's, 452.
— — Aristotle's, 456-9, 495-7.

INDEX. 545

Knowledge, Theories of—
— — Kant's, 404 *sqq.*, 412-5, 423-4, 431-3, 445, 506 *sqq.*
— — Scholastic, 460.
— — Reformers', 461-2.
— — Idealistic, 508 *sqq.*
— Hypotheses underlying, 205, 274, 277, 284.
— Relation between, and science, 386, 412.
— Process of, 394, 412, 457-8, 502, 509 *sqq.*
— Objects of, and thinking subject, 392, 442-3, 446, 463.

Latter Day Pamphlets, 237, 243.
Lavater, 66.
Law, Moral, 417, 418, 419, 427.
— of reason, 420.
Lewes, G., 523.
Leibniz, 70, 322, 383, 465, 467.
Limits, Consciousness of, 443-5, 474-5, 537-8.
Locke, 274, 296, 383, 443, 465, 527.
Logic, Relation of, to metaphysic, 392, 480, 484, 493, 496, 498-9, 510-2.
— and idealistic philosophy, 431, 498, 499, 505-10.
— Relation of, to science, 439, 483, 484, 499.
— Ordinary view of, 480.
— and scholasticism, 482, 488.
— Analytic, 481, 482, 483, 484, 497, 499, 500-1, 509-10.
— Formal, 482, 498.
— Genetic, 499, 509-10.
— of inductive synthesis, 501-4, 509-10.
— Metaphysical, 512.
— Aristotelian, 481, 484, 489, 492, 493.
— Kantian, 508.
— Hegelian, 518 *sqq.*
Logic of Hegel, 438, 517, 532.
Luther, 134, 269.

Maimonides, 382.

Man, as related to nature, 403, 448, 450, 526 *sqq.*
— — to man, 427.
— — to science, 400.
— — to the knowing mind, 449-50, 457.
— as self-determined, 418-20, 467.
— as determined from without, 309, 467-9, 471.
— as a moral agent, 449.
— Natural science of, 471.
Malebranche, 333, 352.
— relation to Cartesianism, 267, 268, 310.
— theory of knowledge, 311.
— relation of the finite to the infinite, 312.
— conception of God, 312, 317, 320, 325, 331.
— Dualism of, 315, 322, 330.
— conception of the world and consciousness of world, 316, 318.
— divergence from Des Cartes, 317.
— criticism on his meaning of self-consciousness, 317.
— nearness to pantheism, 319.
— denial of particular providence, 322.
— conception of will, 324.
— theory of *natural inclinations*, 326.
— use of the passions, 327-31.
— Ethics of, 329.
Mark Rutherford, 194.
Materialism, Kant's relation to, 408.
Matter and mind, Opposition of, 276, 292, 300, 315, 352, 355, 358, 405, 434, 459, 522.
— — Relativity of, 441.
Matthew, 175.
Meditatio tertia, 282.
Meditatio quarta, 290.
Meno, The, 452.
Metaphysic, 384.
— Origin of term, 384.
— Aristotle's conception of, 385-92, 473.

2 M

Metaphysic, Charges brought against above, 389-391.
— Relation of, to natural and spiritual objects, 392.
— Relation of, to SCIENCE, 392-442, 521.
— — in early philosophy, 393.
— — in Socratic school, 395.
— — in Neo-Platonic and mediæval philosophy, 396.
— — Re-action of modern science against scholasticism, 397-402.
— Kant first introduces idea of relativity of thought and being, 404, 441, 469.
— — but confines this relativity to experience, 404-11, 423-6, 428, 429.
— — his dualism, 405, 407, 409-12, 416, 419-23, 431, 434-6.
— — his view of the world, 408.
— — his definition of reason, 412.
— — opposition of pure unity of reason to *synthetic* unity of experience, 412-5.
— — things in themselves viewed as ideals of reason, 415.
— — his equipoise between a thinking consciousness and an empirical consciousness, 416.
— — effort to transcend dualism by means of the moral law, 417-21, 427.
— — Kantian antithesis, 423.
— — its opposite terms essentially related, 425, 469.
— — confusion between unity of formal logic and unity of self-consciousness, 426.
— — the unity of self-consciousness, 428-30, 433-6.
— development of Kant's philosophy, 430.
— — (*a*) attempt to develop a metaphysic based on idea of self-consciousness, 431.
— — (*b*) to show that opposition of thought to its object may be transcended, 431.
Metaphysic, development of Kant's criticism of self-consciousness, 433.
— — opposition of science to its ideals not absolute, 434.
— Fichte's treatment of consciousness, 435.
— — Schelling's, 436.
— — Hegel's, 436.
— unity of science, 437-42.
— Kant and Fichte on function of metaphysic, 438.
— — Schelling, 438.
— — Hegel, 438.
— Relation of, to PSYCHOLOGY, 442-80.
— fallacy implied in idea that science is based on psychology, 443.
— — this fallacy traced to Locke, 443.
— — found in ancient and modern scepticism, 444.
— — also in Kant, 445.
— — rests on a paralogism, 445.
— confusion of metaphysical with psychological problem, 446, 448.
— the separate functions of metaphysic and psychology, 447.
— possibility of a purely objective psychology, 449.
— function of a true psychology, 451.
— its problem first recognised by Socratic school, 451.
— — one-sidedness of Socratic view, 452.
— — partly corrected by Plato, 453.
— — imperfection of Plato's view, 454.
— — Aristotle's criticism of Plato's view, 455.
— — this criticism misunderstood, 456.
— dualism in both Plato and Aristotle, 458.

INDEX. 547

Metaphysic, attitude of Middle Ages towards knowledge, 460.
— — of the Reformers towards religion, 461.
— — towards science, 461.
— religious and empiric consciousness not really different, 464.
— compromise in modern Cartesian philosophy, 465.
— problem of philosophy in modern times, 466.
— is the opposition of without and within absolute? 468.
— — Aristotle's answer, 468.
— — Kant's answer, 469.
— — answer of Kant's successors, 469.
— relation between nature of conscious subject and possibility of metaphysic, 473.
— nature of limits to be transcended by metaphysic, 474-80.
— Relation of, to LOGIC, 480-512.
— — ordinary view of logic, its relation to metaphysic, 480.
— — in mediæval philosophy, 482, 488.
— — in Baconian philosophy, 483, 484.
— Aristotle's division between logic and metaphysic, 484, 493.
— his treatment of business of metaphysic, 485.
— — of relation of intelligence to intelligible world, 480, 486, 491, 496.
— process of thought not simply analytic, 487.
— truth underlying the idea of a formal logic, 489.
— combining of analytic and synthetic elements in thought great difficulty of metaphysic, 492.
— Aristotle's metaphysical theory, 493.
— — its inadequacy, 494.
— he sees thought as *distinction*, not as *relation* also, 496.

Metaphysic, step taken by idealistic philosophy in logical theory, 498.
— thought self-determining, 498, 499.
— relation of analytic, synthetic, and genetic logics to each other, 499-510.
— analytic represents our first scientific attitude to world, 499.
— synthetic represents perception of essential relations between objects, 501-4.
— Hume's criticism of synthetic logic, 504.
— — Kant's answer, 505.
— — its inadequacy, 506.
— genetic logic represents perception of essential relation between mind and things known, 508-10.
— true logic inseparable from metaphysic, 510-2.
— Relation of, to PHILOSOPHY OF RELIGION, 513-39.
— — a first philosophy bound up with a last philosophy, 512-5.
— its explanation of religion, criterion of true metaphysic, 515-7.
— criticism of pure metaphysic of Aristotle and Hegel, 517 *sqq.*
— — of the organic unity of Hegel, 518 *sqq.*
— — objections raised to it, 521, 537.
— arguments for truth of Hegel's position derived from dualism of his opponents, 522 *sqq.*
— rationality of religion must rest on possibility of ultimate synthesis, 530.
— characteristics of Hegelian philosophy, its idealistic view of world and its dialectical movement of thought, 532 *sqq.*
— relation of Hegelian idealism to Christianity, 534 *sqq.*

Metaphysic of Ethics, 427.
Middle Ages, Dualism of, 12, 22, 25, 28, 35, 45, 48, 102.
— Political ideal of, 36, 43.
— Goethe and ideals of, 88.
— Goethe and art of, 97.
Mill, John, 484, 504.
Mind, Limits of, 406, 421, 443.
— Aristotle's conception of, 489.
— Ambiguous use of term, 524.
— See also *Matter*.
Modes, 342, 345, 351, 352, 367, 370, 372, 378.
Monad, Theory of the, 467, 510.
Morale, 312, 316, 329.
Morality, Mediæval, 23, 46.
— its universal principle, 49, 371.
— relation to religion, 50.
— Greek view of, 212, 452.
— how determined, 307.
— its great question, 375.
— moral imperative, 419.
— Spinoza's conception of, 371.
— Kant's conception of, 427.
— Relation of, to consciousness, 473.
More, Henry, 303.
Mysticism, Characteristics of, 395, 435-6, 492.
— Plato's relation to, 480.
— Unity of, 519.

Nature, Goethe's attitude towards, 76, 84, 104.
— — Rousseau's, 118, 120, 160, 171.
— — Wordsworth's, 118, 160, 171.
— — Carlyle's, 255, 257.
— Aristotle's conception of, 389, 396.
— Hegel's philosophy of, 438-40, 525 *sqq*.
— and science, 403, 449, 483, 502-4.
— and man, 403, 448, 450.
— *Return to*, 76, 115, 118, 120, 160, 171, 172.
— *natura naturans*, 84.
Natural inclinations, 326.

Necessity, Law of, 418, 485.
— and freedom, 421, 451, 532.
— in relation to man, 450.
Non-contradiction, Principle of, 427.
Notæ in Programma, 296.
Noumena, 415, 425, 428, 435, 438, 507, 517.
— and phenomena, 405, 407 *sqq.*, 415 *sqq.*
Nouvelle Heloïse, 106, 121.
Novalis, 233.

Objectivity and subjectivity, 464, 468-9, 504-6.
Ode to Lycoris, 175.
Omar Khayyam, 220, 221.
Ontology, 473, 512.
Opinion, 339 *sqq.*, 453-4.
Opposition between the natural and spiritual, 25, 45, 48, 435-6, 438.
— — matter and mind, 276, 292, 300, 315, 352, 355, 358, 405, 434, 459, 522-3.
— — passion and reason, 308, 330, 376.
— — phenomenal and ideal, 398, 458.
— — phenomenal and real, 406, 409, 410, 419, 427, 438, 507.
— — self-consciousness and consciousness of objects, 428 *sqq.*, 480 *sqq.*, 495, 522.
— — a *priori* and a *posteriori*, 456, 465.
— — faith and reason, 460.
— — the given and the known, 506-7.
— — form and matter of thought, 516.
Optimism, Rousseau's, 131 *sqq*.
— Wordsworth's, 188.
— Christian, 216.
Ozanam, 3.

Pantheism, Des Cartes and, 284.
— Malebranche and, 319, 323.
— Spinoza and, 348 *sqq.*, 357 *sqq.*, 372 *sqq.*, 381.

INDEX. 549

Particular and universal, 386, 393-9, 451-8, 458, 493.
Passions, 308, 327-30, 338, 376.
Past and Present, 243, 253, 261, 262, 263.
Perception, 404, 456.
Peter Bell, 178, 181.
Phædo, 395.
Phenomena, see *Noumena*.
Philosophy, Dante's relation to, 5, 8, 38, 48, 50.
— — Goethe's, 65, 68, 72.
— — Rousseau's, 145.
— — Wordsworth's, 153.
— Kantian, 70, 208, 272 *sqq.*, 383, 404 *sqq.*
— Comtian, 197 *sqq.*, 488, 526 *sqq.*
— Aristotelian, 211, 367, 385, 396, 455, 473, 485 *sqq.*, 508 *sqq.*
— Early Greek, 393-6.
— Later German, 430 *sqq.*
— Baconian, 399, 462, 483-4, 504.
— Platonic, 211, 349, 367, 453, 496.
— Hegelian, 430 *sqq.*, 521 *sqq.*
— and religion, 35, 195, 225.
— and poetry, 54-5, 63, 153.
— and science, 153, 192, 225, 228, 396-9, 439, 442, 533.
— Problems of, 59, 63-4, 191, 196, 206, 211, 223 *sqq.*, 351, 385, 393, 442, 454, 466-8.
— of religion, 512 *sqq.*
Philosophy of Nature, 532.
Philosophy of Spirit, 532.
Plato, on Greek politics, 3.
— on relation of part to whole, 6, 63, 395-6, 453 *sqq.*
— on morality, 67.
— and problem of philosophy, 211 *sqq.*, 227-8.
— on opinion, 339.
— on knowledge, 349, 496.
— his idealism, 367.
Poetry, Medieval, 46, 47.
— and philosophy, 54, 63, 153.
— and science, 152.
— Function of, 55 *sqq.*, 153.

Poetry, Spontaneity of, 59.
— Conditions of, 60.
— Wordsworth's conception of, 152.
— Importance of form in, 153.
— relation of form to content, 170.
Positive philosophy, 527.
Positive politics, 527.
Positivists, 205.
Principia, 295, 304.
Puritanism, 106, 235.
Politics of Spinoza, 336.
Prelude, The, 162, 163, 185, 186.
Principium cognoscendi, 284, 304.
Principium essendi, 284.
Private judgment and Protestantism, 136.
— Rousseau and, 142.
Profession of Faith of a Savoyard Vicar, 138, 139.
Protestantism, 134, 136, 144, 173, 461.
— Extreme sects of, 138.
Psychology, Relation of, to metaphysic, 392, 442 *sqq.*, 448, 480.
— Function of, 447 *sqq.*
— as objective, 449.

Ratio, 349.
Real. See *Being* and *Noumena*.
Reason, Rights of, 142.
— Doubt of, 286.
— Demands of, 406.
— Identity of, 406, 427.
— and faith, 460.
— Development of, 468, 470.
— Kant's conception of, 412, 429.
— — Plato's, 454.
— — Aristotle's, 455, 457, 468.
— Practical and theoretical, 417.
— Active and passive, 457, 459.
— Universal and particular, 458.
Reciprocity, Category of, 439, 449.
Reid, 314.
Religion, Ancient, 27, 29, 87.
— Jewish, 27.
— Greek, 212, 215.
— Modern, 221.

Religion, Relation of, to philosophy, 35, 195, 225.
— Relation of, to morality, 50.
— Rousseau's defence of, 130.
— Relation of, to metaphysic, 392, 512-39.
— as objective, 460.
— as subjective, 461.
— and science, 461, 462, 463, 464.
Reminiscence, Doctrine of, 453-4, 457.
Renunciation, Goethe and idea of, 80, 96.
Representative Men, 264.
Republic, The, 3, 211.
Res cogitans, 287.
Res completæ, 341.
Res extensa, 287.
Resp. ad secundas objectiones, 275, 291, 293.
Resp. ad tertias objectiones, 275.
Resp. quartæ, 285.
Resp. sextæ, 295, 299.
Reveries, The, 109, 112.
Revolution, French, 116, 120, 161, 164, 167, 179, 185, 233, 236.
Richter, Jean Paul, 233, 246.
Robbers, The, 89.
Robespierre, 106.
Romanticism, Goethe and, 89.
Rousseau, 105.
— his Deism, 106, 141.
— self-contradiction, 107, 128.
— egoism, 108.
— early influences, 109.
— sensitiveness, 111.
— love of the country, 113.
— Paris life, 113.
— literary career, 115.
— *return to nature*, 115, 118, 120, 160, 171.
— doctrine of good intentions, 117.
— sympathy with the people, 119, 178, 185.
— social contract, 121-4, 128.
— scheme of education, 125, 128.
— individualism, 123, 128, 134, 140, 172, 185.

Rousseau, defence of religion, 130.
— appeal to sentiment, 133.
— fundamental error of, 141.
— mission of, 145.
— *volonté générale*, 125, 128, 135, 141, 143, 185.
— *raison commun*, 133, 135, 139, 141, 173, 185.
— *moi commun*, 129, 130.
— *sentiment intérieur*, 130, 131.
— Comparison between, and Wordsworth, 162, 171, 173, 178 *sqq*.
Rousseau, Morley's, 142.

Sanctuary of Sorrow, 101, 103.
Sartor Resartus, 243, 246, 248.
Scepticism, 206, 214.
— Modern and ancient, 218, 220, 444.
— Scientific, 400.
Sceptics, 200, 202, 205.
Schelling, 71-85, 361, 436, 438.
Schiller, 55, 70, 89, 92, 94, 233, 257.
Scholasticism, 397, 460, 482, 483, 488.
Science and poetry, 152.
— and philosophy, 153, 192, 225, 288, 399, 439 *sqq.*, 483, 491, 533.
— and theology, 219, 461 *sqq*.
— and metaphysic, 392-442.
— and idea of unity, 413, 426, 434 *sqq*.
— and idea of consciousness, 473, 486, 489.
— and nature, 483, 502-4.
— and logic, 439, 483-4, 499, 500.
— and psychology, 443.
— Categories of, 402, 439, 441, 442.
Scientia intuitiva, 349, 353.
Secularism, 220.
Self, Identity of, 409.
— The noumenal, 416.
— and not self, 402, 433, 436, 470, 472.
— Subjective and objective, 426, 431, 447-8, 470.
— Development of, 472.

INDEX. 551

Self-consciousness, as type of knowledge, 445, 494.
— Absolute principle of, 451, 469, 470, 489.
— Definitions of, 472.
— Transition from, to world, 521 sqq.
— See also *Consciousness*.
Shakespeare, 242, 259.
Shelley, 169.
Slavery, 127.
Socrates, 451, 452.
Sonnets on Ecclesiastical History, 166, 167.
Sonnets on National Liberty, 165.
Sonnets on the River Duddon, 157.
Sonnet written near Dover, 155.
Sophists, 213, 227.
Sorrows of Werther, 56, 76, 78, 79, 84, 88.
Spencer, Herbert, 193, 403, 443, 488, 523, 524.
Spinoza, Goethe's relation to, 65, 69, 71, 80, 81, 84, 96.
— his pantheism, 284, 332, 344, 351 sqq., 381.
— relation to Cartesianism, 267-8, 332.
— relation to Jewish philosophy, 332.
— his method, 334-5, 339.
— — its imperfection, 359, 365, 368, 378.
— view of the highest good, 338.
— — of the finite, 388, 853 sqq., 401.
— — of relation between finite and infinite, 357, 360 sqq., 372, 378.
— — of God, 350, 370, 377.
— — of knowledge, 340-4, 351, 401.
— — of opinion, 339, 341.
— — of abstraction and imagination, 341, 353.
— — of thought, 342 sqq., 369.
— — of science, 349.
— — of matter, 353, 361, 369.
— — of relation between mind and matter, 352 sqq., 367-8, 523.

Spinoza's view of evil, 356, 370.
— — of soul and body, 360, 367, 380.
— — of substance, 363 sqq.
— — of relation of the attributes, 368.
— — of morality, 370-81.
— — of will and intelligence, 373, 376.
— — of animals, 380.
— — of relation between reason and passion, 376.
Spirit, Hegel's absolute, 437.
Spiritual Brethren, 41.
St. Augustine, 22, 45, 267, 310.
St. Francis, 47.
St. Just, 106.
St. Paul, 14, 20.
St. Thomas, 45, 48.
Sterne, Laurence, 246.
Star-gazers, The, 155.
Stoics, The, 200, 202, 205.
Summum Bonum, Kant's idea of, 40, 422.
Summa Theologia, 49.
Swift, Dean, 243.
Sub specie æternitatis, 338, 357, 529.
Syllogism, Kant and, 412.
— Aristotle and, 493, 512.
Synthesis, Objective, 196, 197, 203, 208, 224, 416, 425.
— Subjective, 198, 201, 203.
— Philosophical, 200, 205, 215, 225.
Système de la Nature, 73.

Tabula rasa, 489.
Tale of the Tub, 243, 245.
Theætetus, 452.
Thought, Modern movement of, 102, 195, 214, 219 sqq.
— Progress of, 106, 144, 438.
— Three great terms of, 192.
— Universality of, 208, 223, 491 sqq.
— Des Cartes on, 272 sqq.
— Spinoza on, 342 sqq., 369.
— Aristotle on, 486, 493, 495-6.

INDEX.

Thought and being, 274, 276, 287, 404.
— and experience, 405-6, 424, 431, 480.
— and the world, 502.
— Unity of, 406, 412, 424, 466, 492.
— Process of, as analytic, 480 *sqq.*, 493 *sqq.*
— — as synthetic, 491, 498.
— — as self-determined, 498, 509.
— form and content, 480-2, 492 *sqq.*
— Relativity of, 483 *sqq.*, 496 *sqq.*, 510 *sqq.*
Truth, Poetic, 58, 152, 257.
— Scientific, 58, 152, 222, 257, 462 *sqq.*
— Mathematical, 271-2, 279.
— Intellectual, 324.
— Religious, 462-3.
— Errors in, 399.
— Definitions of, 480, 485.
— Relativity of, to mind, 453 *sqq.*, 460.
— *a priori* and *a posteriori*, 401, 456, 459, 465.
Types of Ethical Theory, 303.

Understanding, Perceptive, 412, 508.
— Intuitive, 415, 422, 507.
— Identity of, 512.
Unity, An absolute, 399, 423, 436, 478, 517.
— of self, 404, 426, 433, 469.
— of thought, 412, 424, 432, 519, 520.
— of reason, 412, 413.
— of things and knowing mind, 414, 439, 446, 450, 463, 483, 491, 498.
— of experience, 412, 429.
— Organic, 421, 422, 426, 429, 442, 476, 508-11, 533.
— of self-consciousness and of consciousness, 428 *sqq.*, 477, 508-9, 516, 518.

Unity, Synthetic, 429, 442.
— of knowledge, 508, 516.
— Metaphysical, 512-5.
Unity of Comte's Life and Doctrine, 200.
Universality, 491.
Universal principle, 451-2.
— See also *Particular*.

Vice, Socratic conception of, 452.
Virtue, Socratic conception of, 452.
Voltaire, 73, 114, 141, 144.
Von Hartmann, 521.

Wandering Jew, The, 88.
Wanderjahre, 98.
Warens, Madame de, 113.
Werner, 98.
Will, Human, 419.
White Doe of Rylstone, 178.
Wilhelm Meister, 83.
Wordsworth, 7, 60.
— characteristics of his poetry, 147, 154 *sqq.*, 170, 174 *sqq.*
— vocation, 151.
— conception of poetry, 152.
— place as a poet, 155.
— æsthetic heresy, 159, 183.
— content of his poetry, 160, 170.
— conception of Nature, 160, 174.
— life at Cambridge, 163.
— political changes, 165.
— poetic method, 175.
— Influence of French Revolution on, 162, 164, 167, 169, 179, 185.
— Comparison between Rousseau and, 118, 171, 173, 178, 183, 185, 186.
— conception of man, 179, 185.
— Optimism of, 188.
Wordsworth, Life of, 150.
World, conceptions of, Carlyle's, 256.
— — Des Carte's, 274 *sqq.*
— — Malebranche's, 316.

World, conceptions of, Kant's, 408, 413, 416, 507.
— — Fichte and Schelling's, 436.
— — Plato's, 454, 458.
— — Aristotle's, 459, 468, 490, 516, 522.
— — Hegel's, 521.
— — Spinoza's, 522.

World, conceptions of, Scientific, 484.
— in relation to philosophy, 104, 200, 223, 484, 501.
— as phenomenal, 398, 417, 419.
— in space, 434.
— See also *Consciousness*.

THE END.

GLASGOW : PRINTED AT THE UNIVERSITY PRESS BY ROBERT MACLEHOSE.

www.ingramcontent.com/pod-product-compliance
Lightning Source LLC
Chambersburg PA
CBHW032055220426
43664CB00008B/1003